THE MINDFUL GOLFER

THE MINDFUL
GOLFER

HOW TO LOWER YOUR HANDICAP WHILE RAISING YOUR CONSCIOUSNESS

Stephen Altschuler

SKYHORSE PUBLISHING

Dedication:

To Golfers Everywhere: Learn. Have fun. Stay with it.

Skyhorse Publishing books may be purchased in bulk at special discounts for sales promotion, corporate gifts, fund-raising, or educational purposes. Special editions can also be created to specifications. For details, contact the Special Sales Department, Skyhorse Publishing, 307 West 36th Street, 11th Floor, New York, NY 10018 or info@skyhorsepublishing.com.

Skyhorse® and Skyhorse Publishing® are registered trademarks of Skyhorse Publishing, Inc.®, a Delaware corporation.

Visit our website at www.skyhorsepublishing.com.

10 9 8 7 6 5 4 3 2 1

Library of Congress Cataloging-in-Publication Data is available on file.

Cover design by Jane Sheppard
Cover photo credit Dollar Photo Club
Interior photos by the author
ISBN: 978-1-63220-723-4
Ebook ISBN 978-1-63220-998-6

Printed in China

Contents

The Starter's Hut   **1**
Introduction   1

Hole 1 Waking Up   **7**
What is a Mindful Golfer?   7
The Golfer's Mind   10
The Four Noble Truths of Golf   16
True Gravity   20

Hole 2 Caddie   **23**
Bandon Dunes and the Making of an Honest Golfer   23

Hole 3 Wanting   **33**
A Quiet Mind   33
On Wanting to Be a Better Golfer   36
Taking Inventory   37

Hole 4 Discomfort   **39**
Being Out of Position   39
Golf Will Test You, In and Out   42
Dealing with Poor Shots   43
How to End a Slump   44
Shankapotamous   47
What Golfers can Learn from the 2012 San Francisco Giants   49

Hole 5 Learning   **53**
The Measured Swing   53
The Key Move   57

The Key Downswing Move   60
Impact   63

Hole 6 Improving   **67**
The Challenge of Concentration   67
Owning Your Swing   71
Golf is a Game of Balance   74
The Athletic Golf Swing   77
How to Make a Hole-in-One   80
Building and Maintaining Confidence   83
The Case for Less Practice and More Play   86

Hole 7 Adapting   **89**
What Golf Needs and Doesn't Need   89
Thoughts on the Rules of Golf   93
On Bifurcation: New Suggested Rules for the
    Recreational Golfer   94

Hole 8 Life Lessons   **99**
Guts, Glory, and Plasticity of Mind   99
What Golfers can Learn from Skier Bode Miller   102
The Intimidation Factor   104
Cultivating Patience   105

Hole 9 The Dance Floor   **109**
Rolling the Rock when the Rock won't Roll   109
Reading Greens   111
Zen Putting   114

Hole 10 Swinging   **117**
The Drive: A Journey to Better   117
The Drive: Hit it Hard   121
Align-iron-ment   123
Chipping: Up and Down Re-found   126
Perfect Pitch   128
Course Management   131
Finding and Trusting Your Rhythm   134

Hole 11 On High   **139**
Where Lions Lie with Lambs: The Golf Course   139
Higher Consciousness Golf   142

CONTENTS

Developing Concentration: from Range to Course   145
Golf, as Pure Play, can Heal   149

Hole 12 Seeing   **153**
Slowing Down and Looking Around   153
The Course and the Land   157
At the Home of Golf   159
Links Golf at its Finest: Bandon, Oregon   162

Hole 13 Challenge   **167**
Playing Badly and Staying with the Game   167
The Hardest Thing about this Game . . . and How to
   Take it On   170
Understanding and Using Pressure   172

Hole 14 Class Acts   **177**
Hail to the King: Arnold Palmer   177
Phil   180
Ken Venturi   183
Ernie, Autism, and his Legacy   183
Jack   185

Hole 15 Fall from Grace   **187**
Tiger's Fall from Grace: Meditation and Golf   187
What Golfers can Learn from Tiger   190

Hole 16 The Majors   **193**
The U.S. Open Honored   193
The Masters: Then and Now   197
Stealth Golf at the British Open   200
The PGA Championship: Glory's Last Shot   203
The Ryder Cup: Seve and the Value of Inspiration   205

Hole 17 Why Play?   **209**
Why We Play this Game   209
Hands, Head, and Heart   211
The Last Round of Your Life   213

Hole 18 Home   **217**
Camaraderie: Golf as a Contact Sport   217
As for Golf, Above All, Have Fun   220

Acknowledgments   **225**

The Starter's Hut

AT THE TIME of the Buddha, golf had not yet been invented, but what the great sage discovered when he achieved his enlightenment—namely, The Four Noble Truths—can be directly applied to golf, making the game a vehicle to higher consciousness. The first is that all human beings suffer, a truth felt all too often during any given round of the great game. The second truth is that suffering occurs as a result of desire, and don't all golfers desire to get better? The third Noble Truth is that there is a way out of suffering and that way is a cessation of desire, and don't all of us golfers want to know that way out of suffering, especially in relation to slices, shanks, and finding all sorts of hazards? And finally, the Fourth Noble Truth addresses a way leading to the cessation of suffering via the Noble Eightfold Path, namely, right view, right intention, right speech, right action, right livelihood, right effort, right mindfulness, and right concentration. Applied to golf, that's a lot of "rights" for a game where a lot of "wrongs" can come into play.

Introduction

There is an old Taoist folktale that gets at the heart as to why golf, while being arguably the hardest of games, also offers the deepest life lessons. As heard from the Buddhist teacher and author Jack Kornfield, it goes like this:

A man named Sei Weng owned a beautiful mare, which was praised far and wide. One day this beautiful horse disappeared. The people of his village offered sympathy and sorrow to Sei Weng for his great misfortune.

Sei Weng said simply, "Maybe."

A few days later the lost mare returned, followed by a beautiful wild stallion. The village congratulated Sei Weng for his good fortune.

He said, "Maybe."

Some time later, Sei Weng's only son, while riding the stallion, fell off and broke his leg. The village people once again expressed their sympathy at Sei Weng's misfortune.

Sei Weng again said, "Maybe."

Soon thereafter, war broke out, and all the young men of the village except Sei Weng's lame son were drafted and were killed in battle. The village people were amazed at Sei Weng's good luck. His son was the only young man left alive in the village.

But Sei Weng kept his same attitude: despite all the turmoil, gains and losses, he gave the same dispassionate reply, "Maybe."

My own twenty-first-century version of the story has to do with the nasty cold I caught, skirting the edge of flu season. Oh, that's terrible, my friends bemoaned.

"Maybe," I said.

Three days later I'd made significant progress on this book, having taken sick days from my full-time job. Oh, how terrible that you lost so much time at work and you couldn't go to the gym after work like you always do.

"Maybe," said I.

Turns out, I lost the five pounds I couldn't lose at the gym, because a fever and inactive taste buds made food uninteresting. This play of opposites will go on, I'm sure, like losing yardage off the tee as a result of the weight loss. Oh, how awful, my golf friends will say.

"Maybe," I reply, now safe in the fairway at the 150-yard marker every time.

Golf constantly confronts the player with fortune and misfortune, and the effect each one plays on the mind. Attach to either one, and you're in big trouble. As a result, the game tests you physically, mentally, emotionally, and spiritually. It can lift your spirits like nothing else; or it can send you into the hell realms. It seems silly to non-participants, the brunt of jokes by comedians, and clownish to others, something most U.S. presidents seem to play at great risk of appearing both elitist and klutzy, and a total mystery to most non-golfers who witness their friends and spouses in various states of elation or depression when they return from a day at the course. Even the greatest players are buffeted by this sometime cruel interplay of fortune and misfortune. Amateurs can be absolutely inundated and consumed by that interplay.

In my experience, in over fifty years as a player, about thirty as a meditation practitioner, and forty as a mental health counselor, golf is a game that brings suffering or elation to the surface as no other sport can. It looks innocuous enough, but in a five-hour round, emotions suited to a funeral, a wedding, or serious road rage incidents come into play—particularly the road rage. It brings emotions to the surface faster than any human interaction, calling for an immediate response—a response that somehow needs to clear the slate to allow the golfer to be ready for the next shot, which follows quickly since there are others behind you waiting to play.

In Buddhist terms it requires a complete action and a letting go—both a total involvement and a non-attachment to results. It requires an absorption in the moment, for if memory of the preceding moment intervenes, that will surely muck up the concentration needed to perform the next shot.

It is not unlike the Buddha, seeking freedom from the hindrances of his own mind, sitting under a fig tree fighting off those hindrances, manifested by the goddess Mara, one after the next. And golf has a whole litany of hindrances to contend with, the mind itself being the most contentious. Golf is an outdoors game, subject to the many vicissitudes of climate and weather.

Many of a golf course's defenses—yes, course designers think of it that way—like sand traps and water hazards, are planned with making it hard on the golfer. Many of its defenses are unpredictable like wind and rain. And many play on the mind, triggering reactions that get you to do things you really shouldn't have done—like hit a 4-iron 200 yards over a lake to a small green. OK for professionals, but no, most amateurs wouldn't want to go there.

However, many a weekend golfer would look at that shot, think of what his buddies might think if he played short of the lake, and pull out that club with a prayer attached. He knows he shouldn't attempt it, but his ego shifts into higher gear, challenging his sensibilities, and linking the shot with his identity as a man (women golfers don't usually have these problems).

In other words, golf mimics life like no other sport. It blends elements of the emotional, physical, mental, and spiritual, bringing moments of elation as well as despair. Golf takes courage, faith, skill, patience, restraint, and passion to play it well and continue playing it throughout a lifetime. And you can play golf at almost any age.

Golf can bring out the best in a human being—generosity, courtesy, consideration, kindness, honesty, integrity, camaraderie; or the worst—greed, rudeness, unconsciousness, deception, dishonesty, impatience, and addiction. In the course of one round, you can experience the entire range of human emotions. It is a game that gets in your blood, plays with your mind, rattles your nerves, thrills you to no end, provides deep satisfaction and relaxation, and frustrates you to the point of giving it up entirely.

But do we give it up? No, not usually. We come back. Again and again, filled with hope that this time it will be different, convinced that this time, this next time, we will excel and break whatever score we endeavor to break. And even if we fail, we come back again.

Gluttons for punishment? Masochists? In denial? No. Just human beings who refuse to lie down without a fight.

In daily life, we can avoid, deny, or forestall difficult issues for days, months or years, until they bubble to the surface in divorce, debt, unemployment, depression, or disease. Seemingly small things happen relatively slowly, yes, resulting in big things but quite a bit into the future. In golf the future is always now. The next shot, the present hole, the tree that stymies you, the pond you just dumped your approach shot into. Golf, then, is a Zen sport. If you leave the present moment, you will likely feel the immediate karmic consequences like a hammer hitting your thumb.

HOLE 1
Waking Up

THE WORD BUDDHA means "the awakened one," and the golfer comes closest to this state at the moment of impact with the golf ball, usually a point when the thinking mind stops and a unity occurs among body, mind, spirit, and the delicious senses that arise with that hopefully pure impact.

What is Mindful Golf?

It may be an oxymoron linking mindfulness and golf, but the game is so wedded to success and failure, that it is the perfect venue to practice and train in the great art of being present. In the blink of a flubbed chip, you are challenged to either accept reality and move on with grace or stew in that reality and let it drag you into the ashes. In that chip, you are left exposed, your emotions laid bare for your playing partners to see. There is usually a deep silence after such a disastrous shot, a silence that almost resonates through the cosmos. The black hole of the flubbed chip, sucking all into its vortex. Beings light years away turn their heads toward that silence, noticing the faint gasp of pain uttered by its source.

Pain, suffering, discontent, the skulled or chili-dipped chip, in that moment, hits the chipper like the Big Bang in its moment. How you react is a measure of your level of mindfulness. In fact it may be the closest human beings come to knowing what the Big Bang felt like, and indeed felt equally by presidents, butchers, plumbers, judges, surgeons, and street sweepers: golfers all.

The Buddha said all life is suffering. But he also said there is a way out of life's suffering moments, a way to be free from suffering. So when you do botch a chip, you can learn from it, accept it, and move on. Getting bogged down in that moment, means missing fully living subsequent moments, and that is the opposite of mindfulness. You are trapped in suffering. You drop your club to the ground, you slump over, lowering the brim of your cap, and say, "There goes my freakin' round. I am such an idiot."

Of course, the Buddha never did play golf, nor did he stick with his wife and child, two of life's true tests of enlightenment. We've given him a pass all these years because he talked a good game, and, man, could he meditate. And, oh yes, he chose instead to enlighten all sentient beings. But we have a more direct and immediate opportunity, given the razor's edge of golf. In every round there will be any number of shots that test our courage, our intelligence, our resilience, and our tendency to forget to remember. With each moment, we wipe the slate clean to make ready for the next, as a newborn might, fresh, alive, unburdened by the thought of failure or disappointment in the last.

The mindful golfer is not necessarily an accomplished golfer. Nor is the scratch golfer (i.e., zero handicap) necessarily mindful. The mindful golfer will think well of his playing companions or opponents. She will notice the egret wading in the pond where she just hit her approach. He will acknowledge how fortunate he is to be playing this game even after hitting his tee ball out of bounds. He will feel happy for his playing buddy after watching him sink a thirty-footer, something the Buddhists call *mudita*, or taking pleasure in the good fortune of others.

A mindful golfer will take heed if deer or geese are in the line of his shot, so as to protect from hitting them. And she will take extra care to make sure she doesn't hit another golfer who may be forward of her ball. In other words, the mindful golfer is conscious and aware of his or her surroundings. He keeps his voice down after making a great shot so as not to disturb the concentration of others nearby. Courteous, polite, considerate—these are all characteristics of the mindful golfer.

This does not mean such a golfer does not, at times, get angry, frustrated, demoralized, and even a bit depressed. It's just that he doesn't hold on to these states of mind. She knows they will pass if she allows it.

There is an ingenious and very low-tech monkey trap in South America that consists of a gourd with a hole at one end and a tether attached to the other with the whole deal hanging from a tree. A ball of food is placed in the gourd. The monkey comes along, puts his hand in the gourd, grabs the food, but can't pull his hand out since his fist with the food inside is too big. The monkey hunter comes back and bags the trapped monkey. All the monkey had to do to escape was open his hand and let go of the food to easily pull his hand out of the gourd. But he won't let go of the food, and that is the essence of the trap.

For we golf monkeys, who won't let go of the negative feelings generated by poor shots that can sabotage the next series of holes, all we have to do is let go of the memories of the shots and get ourselves free.

It's very rare to find a mindful golfer. Golf is a game involving desire of such strength it turns into an opiate. You have to find that balance between playing the game and getting gamed by the play. How do you know if you've attained that balance and are moving in the direction of mindful golf? You assess your level of suffering. This takes clear and deep honesty, for Freud has shown us all the ways we avoid that honesty. But you'll know what suffering feels like thanks to those mind states that don't go away so quickly, namely guilt, remorse, anger, fear, and shame.

Hope you find your game . . . and the path that leads to always enjoying it no matter what the shot or score.

The Golfer's Mind

The human mind desires. For a golfer who is standing on the first tee, that translates into wanting to hit it long and straight, setting him up well for the next shot, and ultimately leading to a good score. For the beginner, that desire may just be getting it off the tee and airborne. For the accomplished player, it may be as specific as putting the ball in a certain place in the fairway. It's all "wanting" just the same. So you might ask, "What's wrong with wanting?" Without it, there would be no progress, no ambition, no striving. And it's true: we need wanting and desire to live in this world. But when wanting becomes the end all, be all, of our lives (including our golf game), there is often dissatisfaction. And with dissatisfaction, there is little happiness. And if golf doesn't bring happiness, then why play? Unfortunately, more people then not are coming to that conclusion and are dropping out of the game.

The basis of desire in golf lies in the score, and scoring is a major factor in distinguishing golf as competitive or recreational. If you play it as a competitive sport, keeping score is necessary and desire is essential. Of course, you can view keeping score in a less attached way, but that probably won't win you many tournaments or help lower your handicap. In that case, go ahead and increase the degree of your wanting and be prepared for considerable mental suffering. Just rest assured that all things, including suffering, arise and pass away. Of course they often arise again after a time of more wanting.

For those who play the game more for recreation, I recommend deemphasizing keeping score. I know this may seem heretical to those who consider keeping score sacrosanct, but here's my rationale. The great satisfaction of golfing has to do with making pure contact with the ball, both tee to green and with putting and chipping. There is no other experience in sport like it. That is the element that draws people to the game—much more than attaining good scores, although good scores often follow if pure contact happens consistently. With a pure hit, there is a sound like no other—a whoosh that only the wind outdoes. There is a solid sensation of the contact of ball against clubface. There is the hang time of the ball in the air as it approaches fairway or green. There is the feeling in the hands controlling the club and the flight of the ball. There is the feeling of exhilaration in the mind, in the heart, in the spirit at making pure contact, a feeling that can rarely be put into words.

It is what touring pros feel, and is about the only sport where the amateur can, at times, feel what the pro feels. I made a sixty-footer for birdie recently. I've made three holes-in-one. I've chipped in a number of times. Flew an 8-iron directly into the cup for eagle once . . . when I was fifteen. Tiger Woods made, what Jack Nicklaus called, "one of the most incredible golf shots you'll ever see played" when he pitched it in from just off the green at the Memorial to effectively win the tournament. His feeling then and mine on the previously mentioned shots were not much different in the moment of the accomplishment. It's that kind of game. Of course, Jack forgot to mention his 1-iron at the '72 U.S. Open at Pebble that hit the stick and settled about a foot from the cup for a tap in birdie to insure the win. Again, his feeling over that shot, and mine were different in degree, but not in spirit.

How to get to that feeling of pure contact requires some reining in of the tendency of the mind to want and desire. When Woods hit his "incredible" pitch, I'm sure he was focused on the ball and not on the result of the shot. He studied the daunting challenge, chose his club, took his stance, opened the blade of his club, and judged how long a backswing he needed. But when he pulled the trigger, he was in a world of his own mind beyond any other in the universe at that moment. At that instant, he was beyond desire. He was experiencing what the Buddhists call True Self. Tiger has his faults, sure. Don't we all? But despite his desires, goals, and ambitions, when he strikes the ball on any given shot, he is in this True Self/Golfer's Mind.

At the moment of impact between ball and club, the mind and body need to be in a state of calm, achieved through even breathing, no thought, a connection with the ball via the eye, and execution of the proper fundamentals of hitting a golf ball, only the last of which will you need a pro to point you in the right direction. All the rest, you can accomplish through your own volition, personal practice, and training. Yes, the fundamentals learned from a pro are essential to progress in technique, but learning to quiet the mind and focus on the task at hand is the real challenge.

Taking on that challenge does not involve leaving home and joining a monastery. Devoting some time each morning to sitting still and letting your thoughts settle like filtrate drifting to the bottom of a test tube, leaving clear liquid behind, is a good start. Ten to twenty minutes would be fine. Then every time you go to the range, make that practice ground a form of meditation. You are most often there alone, quietly practicing. It's a tension-free time by yourself and for yourself. Check your fundamentals then focus on the ball before you hit each shot. Do this for ten minutes of your practice session. When you play, see if you can carry over the practice of concentrating on the ball at address. A swing thought (or simple reminder of how to initiate a part of the swing) or two is fine but before you pull the trigger, shut off the thoughts and let your eyes take over without any judgment of what they see. Just the back of a ball, the strike, and looking up after impact to see the result. Success in this case is not where it landed but how it felt. Get used to sensing how it felt after contact and even predicting where it landed based on how impact felt. Get to recognize the feel of when you've hit the ball solidly. Remember, you can still hit it solid and have an off-line result. Your friends or playing companions may not think the shot so good, but you are the final judge, jury, and executioner of how solid you've hit the ball. Only you can tell if you have attained True Self/Golfer's Mind.

The mind cannot be seen nor fully understood, but it is the one element in golf that most influences the performance of the game. I have spent a lifetime examining the mind, my own and others, and have barely scratched the surface of how it works. Most of my insights come via Eastern approaches, specifically through Buddhist meditation and psychology. There is no mystery to these approaches. In fact, they are quite practical and can be demonstrated by examining the minds of successful golfers.

Let's take a look at one of the more successful golfers on Tour, Jason Dufner, winner of the 2013 PGA Championship. Bland fellow, Jason is (ever hear of Dufnering, where the practitioner sits on his hands on the floor, and looks bored? Jason started this trend when he visited an elementary school classroom in 2013), and his golf swing is no better than any other pro out there. But there is a huge difference with how Jason conducts himself on the course compared to his competition, which is not only other players but the course itself. He doesn't worry or even think about how anyone else is doing at any given moment. He just lies back and plays golf and has fun with it. It doesn't look like Jason is having fun, because he may be the least emotional guy in the field. But since I don't know what's in Jason's mind, I will take him at his word that he is indeed having fun. (If you need convincing that The Duf is having fun with golf, see his parody instructional video, "How Duf Does It" from "Funny or Die".) That is a good state of mind for a touring pro, the reason being that he doesn't get in his own way, which is something all of us can learn as well. Because most amateurs do get in their own way, at least as far as golf is concerned, and possibly in other aspects of life.

The problem mostly revolves around negative thinking, something we learn from childhood. Through a series of actions and reactions, we begin to see ourselves as not getting it right. It's what a much different Jason Dufner looked like when he blew a four-shot lead and the playoff against Keegan Bradley in 2012 PGA Championship. It's what I looked like after hitting a great 6-iron fifteen feet from the pin on the par 3 15th at Bennett Valley recently only to 3-putt for a bogey. The first putt was uphill and woefully short, deflating my confidence for the next five-footer and missing it badly. When the first putt is bad, negative thinking can set in for the next and a ton of confidence suddenly drops into a pool of insecurity. In golf, this can happen often within a round, each putt or chip feeling like a looming land mine.

The golfer's mind is like a dog off leash. Anything can trigger it into a spasm of distraction. I laugh at the pros needing absolute quiet before hitting. Noise from the crowd is the least of their worries. The noise in their heads is much more a distraction than any hiccup or camera click. Same thing with amateurs trying to putt while their companions carry on a conversation about their latest business deal. In fact, amateurs might feel less stress on the tee if they knew no one really cared about the results of their shot. To quiet your own mind— and that is where golfers and Buddhist meditators come together— you must first hear yourself talking to yourself, and then tell yourself to shut up. There will always be external noises and sights that you have no control over—crows, people, squirrels, waterfalls, alligators— but the voices within can be commanded to stop. After all, you only need about thirty seconds of silence to accomplish a noise-free shot. Most Buddhist meditation sessions last about thirty to forty minutes of quieting the mind, so performing a golf shot with full attention on the ball is a piece of cake in comparison. It doesn't require any esoteric instruction either. You simply yell "Quiet!" to yourself or "Stop!" in your mind or sub-vocally and return your attention to either your feet contacting the ground, your grip pressure, the sight of a dimple on the back of the ball—anything physical that doesn't trigger any analyzing thoughts. Buddhists call these objects of meditation, and are effective means to accomplish quiet concentration.

Too often, we think of the results or consequences of the shot. How can I avoid the pond? I don't want to reach that bunker. If I hit it too short I'll have a very difficult chip. These are negative thoughts that creep into the mind and affect the body. Such thoughts cause tightness in the body, tightness affects rhythm and timing, and, even for a good player, a shot can stray slightly left or right and wind up in trouble. A golf course is designed with such aberrations of timing in play. It is truly not an easy game.

Of course, there is a time for thoughts on course management. Annika Sorenstam advises standing in an imaginary box behind the ball before taking your address position and thinking through the shot. Once accomplished, you then take your address, clear the mind, and pull the trigger. A few years ago, Kevin Na struggled with starting his swing after addressing the ball, probably the result of too many thoughts invading his head. Great suffering, the Buddhists would say. But eventually Kevin was able to move through this, pull the trigger, and hit often-good shots. He was very open about his process, which I admired, and eventually worked through this traumatic time. He was too talented a golfer to stay stuck for long. Essentially, Na got out of his own way.

So watch your mind. See what it does, how it reacts, what it is saying to you. Take inventory of its content, as the alcoholic would in one of the twelve steps to recovery. For we are all addicts, in a sense, conditioned to our thoughts and how they affect the body. And like other addicts, we need to regain control of those runaway thoughts, especially when swinging a golf club. In doing so, that daunting sequence of well-timed fundamentals will more often synchronize into a well-struck golf shot, and your game will improve.

The Four Noble Truths of Golf

Arguably, golf is just about the hardest sport there is. It tests you physically, mentally, emotionally, and spiritually. It can lift your spirits like nothing else; or it can send you into the hell realms. It can seem silly to non-participants, is the brunt of jokes by comedians, and is clownish to others. It's also a game that many recent U.S. presidents seem to play at great risk of appearing both elitist and klutzy, and a total mystery to most non-golfers who witness their friends and spouses in various states of elation or depression when they return from a day at the course. Even the greatest players, like Tiger Woods (whose mother is a Thai Buddhist, by the way), are constantly tinkering with their swing and paying thousands to coaches to help them. As for amateurs like myself no amount of lessons or practice seems to help.

The game calls for the highest levels of mindfulness, requiring quick, smart decisions, the results of which can result in heaven or hell on earth, experienced graphically in the very next moment. If your attention strays from the moment at hand, you run the risk of suffering immediate negative karma, as the Buddhists put it, piling on even more karma (meaning negative actions) in this lifetime. To make your decisions even harder than the internal ones your own mind creates, there is also wind, cold, rain, damp ground, sun, mud, snow, fog, hills, sand traps, creeks, lakes, ponds, and puddles. There are trees—often lots of trees, densely planted—weeds, reeds, heather, gorse, rocks, and roots. There are fences, forests, bramble, ivy, and oak—the poisonous kind. There are critters like snakes, skunks, deer, geese, and gators—yes, in some places, alligators. Golf is an outdoors game, subject to the many vicissitudes of climate and weather. Many of a golf course's defenses—yes, designers think of it that way—are planned with making it hard on the golfer like traps and water hazards. Many of its defenses are unpredictable like wind and rain. And many play on the mind, triggering reactions that get you to do things you really shouldn't have done—like hit a 4-iron 200 yards over a lake to an elevated green. OK for professionals, but no, most amateurs wouldn't want to go there. However, many a weekend golfer would look at that shot, think of what his buddies might think if he played short of the lake, and pull out that club with a prayer attached. He knows he shouldn't attempt it, but his ego shifts into higher gear, challenging his sensibilities, and linking the shot with his identity as a man (women golfers don't usually have these problems). Golf is an outdoors game but much of it happens between the ears.

So golf offers tremendous opportunities to understand and experience first hand the Buddha's Four Noble Truths and practice the Noble Eightfold Path. The experience is more temporal than unremittingly sitting on a cushion in silence and watching one's mind, body, and breath, but in relation to twenty-first-century American Buddhist practice, temporal may be better. More may stick with it longer.

First Noble Truth: All human beings suffer. In golf, you often realize that truth on the very first tee on the very first hole. You stand there surrounded by others waiting to follow you, your heart is pounding, your hands are sweating, your vision is somewhat blurred, your brain is trying to remember a swing sequence that whole books have been written about, but you can't forget the last time you were in this position and hit the very top of the ball that then traveled all of fifty feet directly to the left into some clump of nasty bramble. Nor can it forget the snickers coming from the crowd, or the silence roaring from your playing partners. It's a horrible experience, as you lay exposed on all levels.

Second Noble Truth: Suffering arises as a result of desire. Golfers above all want to be better at golf. They will read, pay, buy the latest equipment, do anything to achieve that aim. They want better scores. They want to have more fun, and the only way to more fun, they think, is to play better, especially with their friends. They want to hit the ball far, very far. They want to hit it straight at the same time. And all this wanting often is to no avail. They still fail most of the time. And with failure comes, you guessed it, suffering, deep dhukka.

Third Noble Truth: There is a way out of suffering, and that way is a cessation of desire. Golfers see this when they stop keeping score, for instance. They see it when they hit a putt five feet past the hole and in disgust swipe at the next putt, without any thought of results, and it goes in. They see when they have a horrible front nine, practically give up, then have a magical back nine where they can do no wrong. In other words when they give up wanting, wishing, and worrying, they start doing well. The real challenge is to understand this truth while playing the game as it was intended: keeping score, caring about each shot, and clearing the mind to prepare for the next effort, never giving up despite past results. This requires a combination of patience and passion for the game.

Fourth Noble Truth: There is a way leading to the cessation of suffering, and that is the Noble Eightfold Path, namely, right view, right intention, right speech, right action, right livelihood, right effort, right mindfulness, and right concentration.

So now, you are on that first tee, trembling at the thought of anticipatory humiliation, and you change your view of the situation. You rivet your attention on the present moment, where no anticipation occurs. It's just you and the golf ball and the hole before you. Your intention is to strike the ball solidly and cleanly, swinging within yourself at a pace that is comfortable for you and your style. You are thinking good thoughts, positive thoughts of aiming for the right target, not where you don't want to hit it but where you do. You have a set pre-shot routine in place so you're ready for right action. You are playing golf, which is a wholesome game, ruled by decades of etiquette and courtesy, adding to the harmony of the universe without any thought or intention of harming anyone or any being, all of which is known in Buddhist circles as right livelihood. You swing the club with right effort, mindfulness, and concentration; your only goal is hitting the ball solidly, without any attachment as to the results of your swing.

That last comment brings up a key element, and why golf is such an ideal pastime for meditators. If you are attached to the results of your effort, or want them to be a certain way (remember the consequences of wanting or desiring?), you will ultimately suffer. Of course, this is not a bad thing as long as you are aware of what is happening, which brings me to two other mutually interdependent elements: choiceless awareness and a suspension of judgment. Most golfers are keenly aware of what they are doing and where their ball has traveled, but few have no judgment about it. Judgment, of course, leads to desire and its requisite suffering. For a golfer who continues to keep score—and that is an important factor—to play without judgment is a monumental challenge—as much of a challenge as it is for any human being to live daily life without constantly judging oneself, judging others, and comparing oneself to others—all of which lead to thinking you or your situation needs to be different than what it is. We hear the expression "It is what it is" often, but few people really understand what it means or actually practice that little piece of Western wisdom.

Ideally, in golf, we play it as it lies, without consciously improving the way the ball sits on the ground or changing its location (if it's behind a tree, for example). We play the next shot without a thought of the previous shot. We play the course, not the opponent. We clear the mind and swing. When putting, we stay perfectly still, clearing the mind, and moving only the shoulders, arms, and hands. We take our medicine when we hit a bad shot. When we get out of position (like landing in the trees), we put aside heroics and cut our losses, getting back on the fairway as expeditiously as possible. We record our score honestly, with integrity. If we don't keep score—and some don't to reduce the pressure and better relax while playing—we at least play by the rules. We get angry at times, but let it go as quickly as possible, always endeavoring to reduce the time between the feeling and expression of an emotion and letting it go.

Golfers, like monks, keep the body, particularly the head, still; watch the breath, monitoring its changes; are aware of the hands upon the grip, especially the pressure; know where the clubhead is throughout the swing; have good posture during the entire swing; and have a certain swing thought, not unlike a koan that brings the practitioner back to the present moment. And on the rare occasions when you get the swing in the right order, at a copacetic rhythm, and a pace appropriate to how you carry yourself, the results, like a good meditation session, can be very satisfying. Even at times when things don't go so well and the playing becomes skunk golf (i.e., spraying in different directions), the results can be enlightening depending on how you experience it. Buddhists would refer to this as Right View.

So if you want to enhance your meditation practice with an activity in the world that exudes the essence of that practice, golf is the game for you—if you approach it mindfully with an awareness of mind and body. It's a relatively harmless game that provides multiple opportunities—some golfers would say far too many calamitous opportunities—to practice and experience being a human being.

True Gravity

The great and current Champions Tour golfer Fred Couples is completely in balance throughout his powerful yet graceful swing. His pace and subsequent balance approaches True Gravity, that state of being that Michael Murphy coined in his best seller, *Golf in the Kingdom*, where the body is in total connection to the ground, and the mind is at ease and little concerned about results. Golf has so much to do with our connection to the ground. I tried playing the other day in muddy conditions, and it took quite a while before I could adjust to the slippage under foot. Gravity was uncertain and with uncertainty, a smooth, natural golf swing was near impossible.

Uncertainty destroys confidence, and confidence is what golf is all about. That's why the set up is so important: it sets up certainty. In fact the term pre-shot routine misrepresents this aspect of the swing. It is anything but routine. Much awareness and mindfulness must be applied to the set up, for it is the antecedent to an effective swing. And the first sensation in that process is the feel of your feet making contact with the ground. It is the most basic of human attributes: for, essentially, we became a distinct species when we descended from trees and stood upright on our feet. Sorry to say, with the advent of cars and such, it's been downhill ever since. We've lost our ground let alone any sense of True Gravity.

Freddy, Jack, Watson, Hogan, Jones, Player, Trevino, Nelson, and Woods came/come closest, with Woods, since his sex scandal in 2009, losing his emotional and spiritual ground, and woefully falling from grace. Palmer never really came near True Gravity with that slashing swing of his that sent balls in all directions and only won one U.S. Open. (I know: Couples didn't win an Open either, but his swing is so perfectly in balance that he qualifies, hands down, as a practitioner of True Gravity. His fluidness is a manifestation of that.)

So how can we mere mortals attain True Gravity? First, there is an element of the swing that doesn't move, at least not before the swing takes place: the ball. In Buddhist practice, we'd call it the object of meditation. We keep the ball in sight, and, in fact, our object is not to hit the fairway, or green, or hole: It is to hit the ball. That helps keep our head fairly fixed, which keeps our body rotating around its center axis. But if you have the fundamentals down, clear your mind as you gaze upon the ball. And keep watching the impact area after the ball has left your club. Will you hit it flush every time? No. But you will be practicing the art of True Gravity every time. If you continue to practice True Gravity, your results will improve, but True Gravity is not about results. That's the paradox: once you let go of results, there is a greater chance you will achieve the results you desire. It's very subtle though, and something Westerners don't usually get: if the slightest desire trickles in, True Gravity is destroyed and good results smash upon the rocks. That's why it's so difficult to attain. We are a culture of desire seekers and result getters, and it's very hard to break that habit.

So instead of berating yourself over it, you try again . . . and again. In the meantime, it sure beats going to work or taking out the garbage . . . although True Gravity can be attained there as well.

HOLE 2
Caddie

_____

GOLF IS VIRTUALLY the only sport where players are expected to call penalties on themselves. They are expected to be brutally honest with how they approach the game, especially in competition, following the rules impeccably. The same is true on the spiritual path to enlightenment. You are the only judge and jury of your own progress and how honest a look you are taking of yourself. Every step of the way, golf tests you in this regard. The golfer is constantly face-to-face with his or her own mind and own moral code.

This unfolded graphically when I used a caddie for the first time in my life. It was at Bandon Dunes on the southern Oregon coast, a golf resort of some of the greatest true links courses this side of Scotland. It felt like Bobby Jones himself was watching me, and seeing if I would "play it as it lies." Instead, the story unfolds as I felt the eyes of "Disco" Dave, the caddie, upon my every shot.

Bandon Dunes and the Making of an Honest Golfer

Aboriginals want to preserve the first dawning, anthropologists tell us, the first moment of life in the universe, trying to maintain nature as they found it. No embellishments. No improvements.

Nothing to improve. The same goes for Bandon Dunes Golf Resort, consisting of these golf courses: Bandon Trails, Bandon Dunes, Old MacDonald, the thirteen-hole par-3 Bandon Preserve, and Pacific Dunes, the latter designed by master architect Tom Doak. There, it's dreamtime golf on the south central coast of Oregon. These links courses themselves slow you down. It's not that they're hilly, or hard, or long. The courses are all of those. But the lay of the land and sea is so stunning, so mesmerizing, so iconic, your body and mind naturally slow to meet what is before you. The courses want you to tarry, to pause, to reflect, to sit a bit and gaze, to engage in dalliance because their seductiveness won't allow you to do otherwise. The ocean, too—its grand immensity and wildness—slows your pace, and parallels many holes. True links courses, such as those at Bandon, are characterized by rolling dunes lands, mostly tree-less, and often near the ocean. They are defended by wind, weather, sand, hillocks, gorse, heather, and design. They are rare, with only about 160 on the entire planet.

Contrary to this natural inclination of the courses to slow you down, the marshals at Bandon (as do marshals at courses worldwide) speed you up if you dally. The marshals are competent and efficient men who don't understand anything but keeping up and will chastise you if you don't. At Bandon, they are often former caddies who can no longer lug the leather. Their bodies are no longer good for that. So they hunt down intractable golfers and push them like a cattle drive. My caddie pointed two of them out, hiding behind some gorse, keeping an eye on a delinquent foursome, plotting strategy on how to prod the offenders who had apparently gotten too intoxicated by the ocean ambience or the beers in their bags. They had fallen behind a hole, a cardinal sin requiring a stiff reprimand. The whole day can back up, causing the late starters to finish too late, maybe not finish at all, thereby taking their complaints to the general manager, and the marshals don't want to have to deal with the general manager. (I kid the marshals, as Bill Maher might joke. They're actually pretty nice guys. And so is the general manager.)

Two other ways the courses have for slowing you down are sand and wind. Sand lies at the bottom of bunkers that are so deep, wooden steps lead you in and out. You don't want to fly or roll your ball in a bunker at any Bandon course. In war, bunkers are part of fortifications against the enemy. In golf, particularly ocean links golf, bunkers are equivalent to land mines, waiting for the unsuspecting, lurking behind greens and on fairways, camouflaged by dune grasses and ubiquitous gorse, which will also slow you down, piss you off, and almost make you wish you'd taken up badminton instead. The gorse at Bandon contributed to the burning of the town twice in its history. It's tough stuff that has some sort of Mafioso oil in it that burns if you look at it the wrong way. In fact that's how Mike Keiser, owner and founder of Bandon Dunes Resort, convinced the town to build golf courses on pristine dunes on Oregon's treasured coast. He would manage the gorse, thereby reducing the chance of the town burning again. And, in fact, gorse has not been a problem since the courses were first developed in 1999 . . . except to golfers. For once your ball lands in gorse, there are only two ways out: take a stroke penalty for an unplayable lie or pull a Phil Mickelson and try to blast it out. Either way, you're in golfer's jail. The wise will get back to the fairway directly.

Golf, like life, is a matter of staying in a favorable position, and when you get out of position, which we invariably do in golf *and* life, the idea is to get back on track ASAP. At Bandon, you have ample opportunities to test this hypothesis. If the course routings don't get you, the wind, and often the nasty weather, will. The older golfer, myself included, has the added burden of that which he or she is never without: the body. The body doesn't particularly cotton to a golf swing. All the torque and turning, the form and deforming, twisting and stretching, coiling and bracing, dipping and balancing, not to mention impacting and smashing when the club makes contact with the ball, (all of this *and* keeping the head steady?) exacerbates the back straining, the knees grinding, the elbows stressing, the hands vibrating, the neck stretching, the feet lifting, and the arms reaching like an Olympic weightlifter. Golf is not a sport for Casper Milquetoasts. With walking (and at all Bandon courses, there are no power carts—the only options being to carry your own bag, take a pull cart, or hire a caddie), the heart is thumping on the ascents, as those vital elements called timing and rhythm are as available as wings are to a rhinoceros. The golfer increasingly realizes, as time plods on, the hopelessness of his predicament. He attends the gym and does the preventative routines dutifully, but for every joint and muscle attended to, another atrophies. And it is on the golf course or driving range where he or she discovers these new ablations to the body's infrastructure.

Even some of my Pilates-enhanced, genetically gifted, sometimes low-handicapped friends are not immune to the erosive effects of golf. They often brag of their sub-80 rounds to us peasants groveling for pars and bogeys outside the palace walls, but they are haunted by the never-mentioned 85s or 88s or even—don't even think it—92s, evidence that their low-number days are numbered and their awesome distance off the tee is leaking oil. In their case, it is the mind that's showing tiny stress fractures from golf's minute but ubiquitous earth tremors. Can I fly that bunker 220 yards out? Can I clear that gorge across the ocean? Can I make it over that lake just before the green? Can I get there in two? In younger days, these questions would never have come to mind. Why are they plaguing me now, ask the single digit-ers? Why, indeed? The tiny cracks in the musculoskeletal system send imperceptible pulses to the brain that something somewhere is amiss, has changed, and with the change, has not been acknowledged, or worse, accepted and modified. Unsuspecting golfers keep playing as they had before the fissures appeared. They do more Pilates, increase their regime at the gym, practice more at the range, add another golf day to their schedule, only to find the doubts and questions increasing like weeds in a garden that have not been pulled up from the roots. Maladies like golfer's elbow or carpal tunnel syndrome appear, only to be added to that ever-widening river in Egypt: Denial.

These people avoid the links at Bandon. It is safer to remain on their home courses where they've honed their impressive handicaps.

CADDIE

Courses where the wind doesn't blow so much; and you can stay in on rainy days; and the fairways are sixteen-wheeler width; and the rough is cake; and the greens have little break. Bandon and Pacific Dunes are, like all great courses in the world, risky. I really found that out when I played Bandon Dunes the second day out, and, for the first time in my fifty years of golfing, hired a caddie. I had explained to General Manager Hank Hickox that I was having a tough time reading the greens on Pacific Dunes, with putts going in the opposite direction of my read. Maybe it was the ocean or their double-digit Stimpmeter speed or the wrong weights in my two-bar putter, but I had more three-putts than a duck has feathers. So I popped for the added expense and met Dave "Disco" Tatge, or just Dave, at the first tee of Bandon Dunes. It was just he and I since no one else signed up for that time. Dave was probably twenty-six or so, a professional caddie who had worked in Florida, even looping a few rounds for Vijay Singh and Australian Graham Marsh, and he himself a four-handicap, so he told me. His aspirations for working the PGA Tour have lessened lately since he met his girlfriend and her five-year-old. But he's been at Bandon for four years and is quite comfortable there. And, man, can he read those greens! I, on the other hand, could have done as well on my own if I'd putted the ball exactly opposite from what I'd read. Such are greens on a links course, influenced by the ocean, the wind, the malevolencies of the designer, and God, when the Old Testament Bloke really wants to punish us wayward human beings.

Taking a caddie along was about the most intimidating thing I've ever done in my years of playing golf. Think of it as having an extremely knowledgeable gallery of one watching you at a tournament, scrutinizing every move you make, every shot, every club selection, every reaction, every tendency to cheat and give myself a preferred lie on the tight fairways and punishing rough. This last factor was particularly unsettling since I have propped my ball up favorably for many years now, rationalizing the transgression by saying the courses I play are ill-maintained and battered by heavy play. Unlike the pros' manicured courses, they are dog tracks, unfair to the average golfer. So you get to your ball in the fairway, and move it a few inches to a tuft of grass so it props up a bit. No one really sees or notices this as long as you're not playing in a tournament, which I haven't since I was a kid in high school. Your buddies are off doing the same thing to their balls. It becomes a kind of habit, like a prison inmate stealing dining room spoons, or an office worker taking pens and paper for home use, or a housecleaner helping herself to a bar of soap. No big deal. No harm done. Something my consciousness has long since excused as a minor offense in the face of the major problems of the world.

Only one problem with this approach: it ain't golf. Let me say that another way so as not to trivialize my point: it is not, nor will it ever be, a part of the game of golf. There is a rule in tournaments when conditions are so wet and muddy that Clean, Lift, and Place is permitted in the fairways but not the rough, but that is considered a local rule dependant on the conditions of that course and day of play. Otherwise, you have to play it as it lies, or play it down, or play it as you find it. That's what makes golf the sport it is and what makes it so exasperatingly similar to everyday life itself.

A couple times I went to move the ball, but there was Disco Superego, just a few feet away watching my every action. The United States Golf Association personified here as one man keeping the honor of the game intact, at least for these few hours on this Bandon Dunes links course that so typifies the courses where the game was born. Maybe you can improve a lie back home, Buster, but here Dave was bearing witness, like Bobby Jones himself. Go ahead, degrade the game, he was probably thinking. I'll just watch.

My friends, on the other hand, don't give a damn whether I move the ball or not. They just don't want to be confronted themselves for breaking the rules. It's a hard game and getting harder with age: let's just leave each other alone, what with the global financial crisis'n all. We're not hurting anyone. Just propping up our ball to give ourselves an edge. No biggie. But it is big. Huge even, because it undermines a basic trust that golf has with each golfer. It's a big-time honor system sport, perhaps the only sport that works that way. There are no referees for the amateur. No umpires or line judges. Professional golf-ers actually call penalties on themselves, and they do this routinely. Major tournaments have been lost as a result. Imagine John McEnroe doing that, or Mike Tyson, or Roger Clemens, or David Beckham, or Charles Barkley in his younger days, or any other athlete in any major sport. It used to be that the amateur golfer was the paragon of honesty, maintaining the great values of the sport more that the pros. In the days of Bobby Jones and up to the early 1950s, the amateur golfer was revered for always acting with dignity, honesty, and integrity. I think that still holds for the tournament-playing amateur, but the everyday golfer, who in some ways represents the future of the sport, has gotten into the habit of cutting corners, of kicking his ball away from a tree, of preferred lies in the rough, of dropping a ball that has gone into a water hazard making it seem like it came up short, of marking the wrong score on his card, of resetting his ball marker on the green a few inches shorter, all sorts of transgressions to make it seem he's a better golfer than he is (and I suspect it is men—of the rumpled ego—who do more of this than the average woman golfer, but that's just a hunch).

So there I am on the par 4th hole at Bandon Dunes, in golfer's jail with a lie in the rough like spaghetti, where the only legitimate way out is to waste a stroke and chip it out to the fairway. I was ready to prop the ball up to the top of the grass with my club, to give myself, what we amateurs call, "a preferred lie," laughingly legitimate in the fairway but totally *verboten* in the rough. Dave was slightly behind and looking back at the foursome behind us, checking its position, and seemingly out of sight. I reached out but stopped my arm from acting. Something inside of me, first the thought of Dave seeing the offense, then a voice whispering in my brain, "That is not within proper golf procedures and rules, buddy boy." So I stepped away, reas-sessing my predicament now that I surmised there was no way out but to leave it as it lied and thrash my way out.

"I think you'll need to just chip it out onto the fairway," said Dave, in a tone a doctor would use to pronounce a dire diagnosis. "Get it back in play."

"Yeah, looks like," I replied, going through Kubler-Ross's five stages of grief in about ten seconds.

So I did, and lost a shot, but I was out safe and had retained the integrity and dignity of the ancient game of golf. I was dead, but golf was alive. After more of this, I began to internalize the play-it-as-it-lies rule and gradually began to see why it was initiated in the first place a few hundred years ago on the sheep farms turned golf courses of Scotland: it equalizes the playing field. Everyone plays under the same conditions, so what is measured are the playing skills of the players themselves. Other than skill, one player does not have an advantage over another by taking a better lie. I do bend the rule in the winter in the mud of northern California, but so do the pros on occasion with their "clean, lift, and place" rule in sloppy conditions.

What I found upon continuing this first round of honest golf since I played in tournaments as a teenager was that I enjoyed the challenge. There was no decision or action to be taken with the lie of the golf ball. It just stayed where it landed, and if it landed in an unplayable situation, like near a tree root or rock, I took a penalty or free drop depending on the universal or local rules. The only decision I had to make was how to play the shot. Somehow, this was comforting, even though the shot might be more difficult as a result of not being able to move the ball into a better position. I had the USGA, in the guise of caddie Dave, to thank for all of that, something he had no idea he helped me work through. I gave him a better-than-average tip for doing his job in carrying the bag, reading my putts, and defending the honor of golf.

Back home, after Bandon, I continued playing in this way and wish I could say I played better, but I didn't. The tight lies still confound me, but I was able to concentrate more effectively, dealing with the lie only when I approached and saw the ball. At Bandon, the fairway lies were tighter than Madonna's you-know-what. But I got fairly good hitting off those lies and not worrying about them as I had in the past on tight lie courses around home. This was particularly true with hybrids and fairway woods, so now, at home courses, I just walk right up and figure I can handle any lie reasonably well. I sometimes top the shot, but more and more, I hit it square. And I feel a sense of pride that I haven't felt before.

Same with the wind. If I could handle two and three club winds at Bandon, which I did, I could manage anything the San Francisco Bay Area could throw at me. Once you play links golf by the ocean, all future wind becomes relative to that ocean links wind. It's a matter of holding your balance throughout the swing, gearing down to about 80 percent, and then figuring out how much more or less club you need. Piece-o-cake. Well, maybe that's hyperbole, but wind doesn't concern me as much. If it stays fairly constant around speed and direction, I choose the club depending if the wind is with or against me. No problem. And, I'll tell you, a solidly hit shot with a swing and a body in balance, defies the wind. You learn quickly, too, to keep the ball down and play knock-down, run-up shots, and putt from 20-plus yards off the green, and leave your wedges at home.

So am I a better golfer? No, not really. My handicap is still doing 10 to 12, with no chance of parole anytime soon. But my attitude toward the game is better. I choose not to pound as many practice balls, which abuses my aging body. I go out for my once-a-week game with more a sense of play than ambition, with a swing that strains at the joints but held up pretty well at the toughest golf of all: links golf by the sea at Bandon and Pacific Dunes. And I think I can hang with that swing until the next seismic change to my body. Then I'll gear it down a bit, letting those high-tech clubs do their thing.

I do know that I am a truer golfer, for I now play it as it lies . . . and that's no lie.

HOLE 3
Wanting

FOR A GOLFER, wanting to play better usually means desiring a lower score, an uncertain road that can lead to fortune or misfortune. Still, the word "play" is paramount, and, when I experience the game as pure play, I am in a different world than my work-a-day life, now focused on the playing field, my companions, and the interaction of my mind and body. Away from the freeways and flashing lights of the city or town, I am totally relaxed yet vibrantly awake as my feet make contact with Earth. I am aware of all my senses much more so than other busier times during the day. I can still "want" but in a much healthier context than "normal," and changes that I once considered mundane can transform into the realm of the extraordinary.

A Quiet Mind

The human mind is unique in nature. The brain can be compared to other species, can be analyzed, tested, inspected, preserved, and bottled. But the mind . . . well, what in the Sam Hill is it? You can't see it, hold it, test it, or even know it that well. But in golf, we get to experience it almost every time we address the ball. And at golf tournaments, we can almost catch a glimpse of the minds of every participant. "I've played this event where I've been very tense and other times I've been quite calm," said Ernie Els after round two of the U.S. Open at Pebble Beach a few years ago. "And all I can say is that the times that I've been tense, my game wasn't quite there. And there's so much trouble that you've got to stop thinking about it. This week, I'm feeling all right."

Players, even those in your weekend group, watch each other closely—how they react after good and bad shots, not looking so much at their swings, but their minds. For the mind is always adapting to the ever-changing conditions confronting the golfer. At a U.S. Open, those conditions are formidable, growing increasingly challenging as golfers wade into the weekend. And the mind is ever susceptible to those added pressures and environmental changes. But how many golfers exercise the mind as they do their swing? An addled mind can change a swing—its tempo, pace, and rhythm. A swing off just a millisecond from its normal pace can translate into missing a green, which, at a place like Pebble Beach, can spell disaster.

Exercising the mind means quieting the mind. No easy feat. The thinking mind is like a gyroscope: it just keeps spinning, reacting, judging, worrying, and analyzing. In golf, as in most of the rest of life, these are necessary tasks. But at the moment of action, particularly in golf, the mind must stop its activity and come to a place of quiet and peace. Any uncertainty or doubt about the decision regarding the shot ahead will translate into some aberrant behavior that will manifest somehow through the body. Maybe the backswing will not be completed. Maybe the hands will prematurely start the downswing out of sync with the hips and legs. Maybe the head will lurch a bit forward as the body heads toward impact. Maybe the big toe on the right foot will twitch. Who knows all the details that take place during a golf swing? But you can bet that the source of the twitch or lurch or pull was something that was happening in the mind, just prior to pulling the swing trigger.

So I have three recommendations: (1) develop a meditation practice to get your mind used to being quieter; (2) when you address the ball have just one simple swing thought in mind (mine, at least for the moment, is keeping the tilt of the spine the same through impact); and (3) swing. In other words, don't take too much time over the ball once the swing thought is firmly in mind. Just swing, and let the chips fall where they may. You've done your preparation on the range and on the meditation cushion or chair, and now it's time to align your body toward your target and trust your swing.

The results? Well, all the best to you, but whether they are good or bad, you've done your job, as my buddy Ed Biglin always says. You've speeded up play. You've had a moment of peace during the swing. Now wipe the slate clean, find your ball, and repeat the procedure. Over time, you'll improve, and you might even gain some control, like Ernie Els has, over that non-stop mind.

On Wanting to be a Better Golfer

Ambition and desire play an important role in golf and make it very difficult to stay present with each swing. For with each shot, we want some result, as we do in daily life with work, relationships, health, recreation, shopping, etc. Great sages such as the Buddha, Krishnamurti, and Jesus discouraged ambition and desire, claiming these led to suffering and discomfort. I've experimented with this and discovered that what they said was true. But these characteristics form the basis of our Western society and must be considered. So, as a golfer and as a human being, what to do? Do we stop wanting to accomplish things? Do we delude ourselves into thinking that we have no desires and any result is OK? Something like, "I don't really care how I do. As long as I'm out enjoying the sunshine." Yeah, right! First, be honest: we do want things to happen in certain ways. We really want that 7-iron to clear the bunker in front of the green and softly land ten feet from the pin. Damn right we do. But what happens if we plug in the sand? How attached were you to the results of the shot? How angry do you get? And how long does that anger stick around?

Attachment is not all or nothing. There are degrees of it. The more attached you are to results, the more frustrated you will become if the desired results are not attained. And psychologists tell us frustration leads to anger. And once anger enters the mind and then the body, it's hard to subdue. In his prime, Tiger Woods got angry when he hit a wayward shot, but he let go of that anger before he reached the next shot. Tiger used his Buddhist background and training in this regard. He let the anger out, usually in the form of slamming down his club or cursing or scowling, then walked on to where the shot landed, and began his assessment of his situation. The emotion could be acknowledged and released in the mind without anyone knowing what is happening inside the head. Hogan was a master at this. Jack Nicklaus rarely showed much emotion when he missed a shot. And Arnold just charged ahead, found his ball, and hit some amazing recovery shot, without ever revealing any anger over the shot that got him into trouble. These three certainly wouldn't curse or throw tantrums the way Woods did. Bobby Jones didn't become the great golfer and the great individual he was until he gained control over his anger.

So you need to try to improve while keeping the game in perspective, namely that it's a game and that the results of your round don't really mean much when compared with other more vital issues. It means something to your ego alone, and your ego's not worth throwing a tantrum over. Whatever the outcome of your round, let it go. If you've done poorly, go to the range and work on whatever it was that didn't work. If you did well, play again as soon as possible and see if you can repeat what you think you did right. Try to neither berate nor praise yourself. Just see if you can learn something about yourself.

Taking Inventory

Golf may be the most demanding game/sport there is. You're faced with a series of shots that lead to results that add up to a score that measures how you're doing. If you let a poor shot remain in your mind when you play a subsequent shot, you will be unable to fully concentrate in the moment of that present shot. If you remain angry, judgmental, regretful, dejected, embarrassed, or a whole range of other negative mind states, your next shot will probably suffer and your score will reflect it. The game is unforgiving in that way. And so, not only do you need to practice the physical aspects of a proper swing but also you need to take inventory of how your mind reacts to the results of those swings and make changes as needed.

HOLE 4
Discomfort

G **OLF CONFRONTS US** with discomfort all the time. It's part of the challenge of the game. But as the Taoists say, "Within every challenge is an opportunity." You will be out of position often while playing this game, and how you relate to those times reflects on how you relate to discomfort generally in life. For success in golf, and life, is determined more by how you deal with discomfort than comfort.

Being Out of Position

In golf, as in life, the idea is to stay in position, to keep the ball in play, even at the expense of distance or too much success too soon. Otherwise, you're always struggling, always making up ground, always losing strokes just to get back in play, always taking two steps back for each forward. For a touring pro, he may look up one day, perhaps in his forties, and realize he has not really succeeded in his chosen profession. He has been out of position a bit too often, to the point where that has become the norm. It's what he knows best and is almost too comfortable with being there. John Daly and Paul Goydos come to mind. Steve Stricker, on the other hand, on the brink of quitting the game after years of being too out of position, fought back to become

Number 2 in the world at one point. For the amateur, being out of position, too, may have become too familiar. His expectations begin to slide. He loses hope that his game will improve. He talks himself into believing he's just out there to have fun and that's enough for him. Even in business or marriage or health, he has slipped into always being a bit out of position, and settled into that state of being slightly out of balance, more or less. A frustration hovers like a fog, which develops into a mild depression, malaise, stagnancy, and subtle contentment with mediocrity.

And yet, there is a danger in not risking, in staying too safe, in laying up instead of "going for it." So to play golf and always endeavor to stay in position by playing it safe is not the Seve Ballesteros approach—a way of passion, *joie de vivre*, and adventure. Risk must not be without some restraint, though. It must be calculated, not foolhardy. If you have 220 yards to clear a lake to reach the green and all you've ever hit your 3-wood before is 210, it would not be wise to attempt the shot. Laying up in the fairway and having a short wedge left could lead to birdie or par and not the double bogey a ball in the lake might bring. Your playing partners might ridicule you for laying up, call you "Alice" and such nonsense, but they are not playing your game, nor are they living your life. Some TV commentators often criticize pros for laying up when they thought them capable of reaching the green. But they were not there, and they weren't inside the heads of those guys who knew a whole lot more about what they were confronting.

The difficulty we get into in golf, and in life, has to do with the ego's tendency to want to be at center stage, to shine, even when faced with evidence that would indicate probable failure. Another word for this is denial. We don't want to face the reality that since we've never practiced the shot at hand, we might not be prepared to pull it off; or even though we've never sold cars, we could still be a successful car salesman. That could be a good trait under certain circumstances, displaying a confidence that could surmount inexperience. It could also be a stupid one.

DISCOMFORT

So in golf, and in life, we are constantly assessing our present situation, more intensely than we realize, and *vis-à-vis* our desires for the future. Golf is a great training ground for life decisions as we have many opportunities in the span of an 18-hole round to practice how we make decisions. And they pop up quite quickly. We have just a couple minutes when we reach our ball to take many things into consideration and decide how we are going to play the next shot. Is there a hazard to take into account? Wind? A poor lie? A bunker? As a golfer, you're well aware of all the possibilities. But even more so is how your mind relates to those obstacles. Apprehension, fear, annoyance, regret, anger, relief, happiness—we are conditioned to feel an emotion according to the past connection we have with each obstacle. And, in a general way, we are either confident our swing and skills can handle particular hazards, or we are not; or we're somewhere floundering in the limbo of doubt and uncertainty, which is probably where most amateurs are, more or less.

In life, it's easy to delude ourselves that we are in position when we are not. The ego is very clever in this way and knows all the tricks of deception. We are easily fooled. There are countless examples of well-known people who deluded themselves into thinking they could get away with all sorts of transgressions but ultimately put themselves woefully out of position. In golf, we know immediately when we are out of position during a round, and, for a pro, during a career. David Duval, struggling with a back injury, fell out of position around golf (his family life has blossomed, however) about nine years ago and is desperately trying to get back in form, showing occasional flashes of his former skills. Adam Scott, before he won the Masters, was performing far below his capacity and was consistently out of position with his game. New Zealander Michael Campbell, after winning the U.S. Open in 2005, has fallen off the charts, and his career is slipping away. At present, he is seriously out of position. For most golfers during an average round, we know when we've had to waste a shot to get back in play, or when we've tried the so-called heroic shot over, under, or through trees, for example, and run into more wasted shots. With time and experience, we learn when to "take our medicine" and chip the ball back on to the fairway, and back into position.

The automatic pilot of an airplane is always a little off course but eventually gets the plane to its destination, right on target. Being off course is part of the norm. It's similar with golf, since we seldom hit the ball exactly where we want it. If we weren't out of position at times, we'd never experience the thrill of being in position, which is what makes golf such an exciting, intriguing, and satisfying sport. So don't curse the times you are out of position. Honor them, and like Arnold Palmer of old, go find your ball, and without complaint, assess your situation, plan a strategy, focus, and get it back—in his case, thrash it back—into play. It worked pretty well for him—in golf, and in life.

Golf Will Test You, In and Out

Golf is a game that will test you repeatedly—physically, emotionally, even spiritually. It will test how present you are with your moments and how readily you can let go of the outcome of each moment. You haven't much time to process the results of the moment, namely the last shot. You have several minutes between shots depending on their length. What happens in your mind during that walk/ride to the next shot will determine your preparedness for that shot. In this way, a round is built and developed. Like a builder who must be impeccable at each stage of the foundation and framing, you must be able to put the last shot behind you and proceed to analyzing the next.

That's why it's the most demanding game/sport there is. The score is an indication as to how you're doing. It's not the whole story but gives a barometer of how your mind works in relation to your body. So to improve in golf is not only to work on your swing and how your body performs it but also to watch the workings of your mind and what you tell yourself. Are you a harsh critic? Do you berate yourself continually? Do you obsess on the past, especially the immediate past? Do you wallow in self-pity and judgment? Are you having fun? You might apply these questions to your life as well, and take inventory with the intent of making changes.

Dealing with Poor Shots

One of my golf buddies often laughs when he mis-hits a shot. It's a strange, almost macabre laugh, like that of a deranged man being led to the gas chamber. Golf can bring that out. It is definitely not a laugh of joy, or delight, or whimsy. There are a lot of tears in that laugh, and the louder he laughs, the more anguish is beneath it. It's a laugh that makes me feel uncomfortable, for no one else around us is laughing with him. We all have our heads down and no one is looking at him as he looks at the club, then at the ground, then in the direction of the wayward ball. We've all been there . . . except for the laughing bit. Hunter Mahan laughed some too when he flubbed that chip on the last hole in the Ryder Cup a few years ago. What else could he do? The crying would come later. But at the moment of the misstep, all he could do was smile. He just lost his match and probably the Cup— the chili-dip heard round the world . . . probably for years to come in highlight reels. Maybe the smile softened the blow of the embarrassing moment. For my buddy, too, the laugh, I guess, softens the blow of the feeling of despair after the shock of the shot.

So how to deal with poor shots? They *will* happen . . . to all of us: pro or amateur, expert or dub. We all know, with a sense of dread, they can all happen during the course of any round. Having been a mental health counselor and a Buddhist meditator most of my life, I know that feelings must be expressed but not dwelt upon, felt but not indulged in, identified but not over processed. We've all seen Tiger curse a bad shot then cozy a 6-iron three feet from the hole on the next shot. Whether you like him or not, the man does have the ability to express what he feels then let it go. He trusts his ability to come back from a bad shot, clear his head, bear down, and make the next shot with full concentration. He trusts his physical conditioning to perform at a level called upon. We've also seen what can happen to

Tiger when he is too distracted by events off the course that have become out of control through his own doing. The concentration needed for his level of play is not fully there.

When you haven't the time to play regularly, the golf swing you've used to play well in the past may no longer be as available to you as before. And the more you try to remember and return to it, the more tension you create in your body and mind. And the more tension, the more likely it is you will hit poor shots. So instead of rushing to the course to make your tee time with no practice, no stretching, no reviewing swing thoughts, no deep breathing, you need to get to the course early, hit a bucket to find your swing for the day, hit some chips to find your chipping stroke, and spend some time on the putting green. You can do this if you get up early enough and plan your time accordingly, as you might for work or to get to a doctor's appointment. Despite what your spouse might think, preparing for a day of golf is just as important.

What I'm suggesting for us players who don't practice enough between rounds is that, yes, we have a different swing each time we play a new round—perhaps not fundamentally different, but different in timing, tempo, and the condition of our body and mind on any given day. And as we age, the differences get more dramatic. If you practice before the round, at least you can go back to the memory of the practice routine to re-find your swing for the day. So instead of fooling around looking for different elements while you're playing, you now have a baseline to which you can return. Does it always work? Hardly. But when it doesn't, at least you can thank God you don't play this game for a living.

How to End a Slump

Yani Tseng, from Taiwan, a few years ago the number one female golfer in the world, found herself in the middle of a terrible slump, which toppled her from world number One a few years ago. It was a sad thing to watch. This great golfer, and great person, not too long ago dominated the LPGA tour. She was predicted to win just about everything she entered. I would say she was more dominating than Annika Sorenstam was in her prime. In 2014, she showed signs of rejuvenation, but Yani is still in a slump and hasn't had a win in a long time.

"I feel I'm happier and enjoy life more instead of trying to worry about world number one or winning the tournament," she said. "I just want to go out there and have fun with everybody else and try to make birdie every hole, and if not, go to the next tournament and try to play well. We still have more tournaments and next year to come."

It's that attitude that makes Yani so endearing and has me pulling for her to find her form again.

The slump. Any of us who've played golf long enough have experienced a slump, feeling like we'd never get out of it. For a slump untreated, like an infection, can lead to a more serious illness. Whereas a slump treated will hasten the healing process. First thing then is to take a proactive stance and treat the condition rather than let it run its course. In golf, it won't necessarily go away by itself. Try the Zen approach, meaning you go into the heart of the matter without over-thinking it. You hold the slump up to the light. You look at it like a crystal from all angles. You feel the slump in all its changing forms. And you take some initial action. My suggestion is to spend time on the range and not play the course for a while. For what you need is to confront your relationship with golf, in a broad-brush sense, rather than a surgical approach, cutting and probing and dissecting and video taping ad infinitum.

For a slump is like a depression: it has been brewing for a long time before it appears as something you are aware is a problem. And like depression, before you can do something about it, you need to acknowledge it as a problem. From Yani's statement about being happier and having fun, it seems she is not quite there yet. You've got to go into the depths of the kitchen and sift through the ashes. You see, the slump is more a teacher than an adversary. We think it has developed to lead you away from the game, but really, the slump shows you a pathway toward more intimacy with the game. You love this game. It is part of your life. It is a source of much joy and fun. But there is a deeper aspect to golf that must be acknowledged—an aspect that transcends desire, ambition, and pride. The great world teacher, Krishnamurti, was a golfer, and I'm sure knew of golf's ability to take one into deeper realms of consciousness. And if you're not aware of the need to come face to face with golf in this context, then a slump will remind you, as a depression will remind you, of the need to explore your inner life more fully and comprehensively.

Golf as guru. Most other sports take you to the edge of ecstasy but not beyond. And it is this quality of "beyond" that golf offers as a gift. Accept the gift to explore this territory, and you take on the journey of a human being, being truly human. Reject the gift and you reject the deeper essence of golf as a metaphor for life. Most reject the gift, settle for golf as yet another endeavor to be achieved, and eventually experience discomfort, a more useful term than the Buddhist reference to "suffering," which can avalanche into a slump.

So what you want to do on the range is attempt to hit the ball on the sweet spot as much as you can. You'll know if you've done this by the sound the ball makes when it leaves the clubface. There is sight too, as the ball will hang in the air suspended in a kind of blissful slow motion before it descends to earth, featherlike. This combination of sound and sight of a well-struck golf shot can lead you into a higher and deeper intimacy with the game. Of course, you'll want to continue on the range until you can experience this consistently. Be patient. This could take days, weeks, or months. Legend has it that the great Hall of Famer and now TV commentator, Lanny Wadkins, shot 79 the first round he ever played as a youngster. How? He became intimate with his golf swing on the range before ever trying it out on the course.

So find a range with grass tees. You'll eventually hurt yourself hitting too many balls off artificial mats. If you can't hear and see what I'm describing, find a pro you can relate to and take enough lessons to get the fundamentals down. Golf takes precise rhythm and timing so you have to know what you're doing and why. Listen to the ball off the club and watch its flight. When you achieve what I've described consistently, go to the short game practice area and make sure you can hit the sweet spot when you chip and putt the ball as well. Doesn't matter where it goes. Just hit the sweet spot, hearing that lovely ping when it leaves the clubface.

Now, go play. Chances are your slump may be over, or, as Leonard, the Native American shaman on TV's *Northern Exposure*, always said, "Or not."

Shankapotamous

When the shanks come, they are as shocking as what I imagine a home invasion must be like. Suddenly the ball is flying off at right angles. Profanities roll off the tongue like a drunken sailor. You take a few practice swings, disbelieving what just happened. It happens again. You put the club down, hoping the affliction will pass like a thunderstorm in the night. Kaboom! A thunderbolt above, then a flash of shank, the very word sounding like a knight in heavy armor lanced, or shanked, through the neck, falling from his trusty steed. Shank, the very word rattling the confidence of a well-tuned swing, putting in place thoughts of doom, dread, and draconian measures to extract the beast, the cur, Mephistopheles himself. Golfers don't even want to utter the word, like *cancer*, for fear they will catch it. The S word, indeed.

That's it: it's over—the goals, the hopes, the handicap. The crucifix of shank. Every subsequent shot is stained with the caustic thought and image of shank, approaching near phobic proportions. There is nothing that rivals the feel of a well-struck golf shot: there is nothing that rivals the jarring feel of a shank (think Kevin Costner in the film *Tin Cup*). And they can occur within one round, indeed from one shot to another. They come, like an earthquake, completely unannounced, and, to the unsuspecting golfer, completely devastating. Like me the other day.

They entered my swing like a drone, far under any radar, attacking after a series of very good, solid shots. I was at the range with my golf buddy Steve, and thank God he was preoccupied giving instruction to a neighbor's son (God help the boy!). If he'd seen my machine gun series of shots, from driver to wedge, he would have laughed that macabre laugh of his like when he misses a three-foot putt for par. I tried to modify my stance, slow my swing down, lead the downswing with my hips. Nothing worked. Shot after shot, the ball careened off the hosel like a tilted pinball machine, witnessed only by me. What the hell was going on? For hell it was, a true definition, a man-made condition that exists solely in the mind of the human being who created it. Rung by rung, I descended into its depths as each shot shanked. Eternal damnation in the Inferno. Just as hell formed the basis of a religion to keep people in line and continuing to drop donations into the hat, it got me ready to sell my soul for a way out. Dante and Faust were surely golfers. As the precocious baby in the TV commercial so critically, yet humorously, points out, I had become a Shankapotamous.

So how did I extricate myself from the ravages of shank hell? I did a few things: I set up about an inch farther away from the ball, lining up the club a bit toward the toe side of the sweet spot; I kept my head steady throughout the swing, clearing my mind of any thought of a shank result; and I shortened my backswing a bit, setting the wrists earlier than usual particularly for the irons. The shots started flying more left than I wanted, but at least they weren't shanking. Hitting a series of 7-irons, slowly my confidence rebounded. And by throwing my arms out toward the target at impact, the shots began to straighten out. The shanks were gone, but the memory lingered.

Part of why they came is that I am unable to play as much golf lately as I'd like. It's called life, the life of a working stiff who is married with responsibilities. Golf requires play and practice. It's a game of intricate, fine motor manipulation and skill. Any change in routine, any nuance of set up or impact position, can result in disaster. The touring pros go to work each day at the course or range, as I go to work at a large state office building. They are able to keep the swing running like a fine car, humming through the ball with correct pace and rhythm. Freddy Couples comes to mind, in his early fifties, still hitting the ball over 300 yards with his bad back. Luke Donald makes few mistakes, he said, in his life of golf. He keeps the body fluid with practice and exercise, the mind clear with his artwork, and the spirit alive with wife and children. He's the whole package. Does he worry about shanking? I suspect not.

Although what golfer doesn't worry about the infamous shank? We all know it could happen at any time. We've probably all experienced it at one time or another. Or if not, we've read about it. In light of this, I'd recommend practicing and warming up before you play. I know this a chore and a bother most of the time. We get to the course late, our tee time is on us like a supervisor at work, we have to finish in time to go to dinner with our spouse. But the only way to insure you're ready to play is to know what swing you bring to the course that day. And the only way to do this is to get to the course early enough to hit the range and see what's doing. That way if a shank did creep in, you'd have a better chance of correcting it quickly. Swings, like emotions, do change from day to day for an amateur. And you need to have the flexibility to go with that swing instead of trying to force it to change according to what you think it should be.

A shank is not the end of the world, though it may feel that way. You can work it out and correct the errors. They're not really that complicated, as I've pointed out. Step back, literally and figuratively. Clear the mind, and swing again. You can do this, Shankapotamous.

What Golfers Can Learn from the 2012 San Francisco Giants

After the San Francisco Giants won the 2012 World Series, outfielder Hunter Pence said this team just never let doubt enter their minds. It's good advice for a baseball team, and it's good advice for a golfer, amateur or pro. Dire situations can turn around like a ballet dancer, pirouetting into something positive. The Giants had their backs to the wall a number of times that season, looking dead in the water around midsummer. Somehow, they toughed it out to make the playoffs. Then they battled back from six elimination games—those were six games they had to win to avoid elimination—against Cincinnati, and again against St. Louis to survive to the series, where they swept away Detroit like Johnson took Goldwater. No contest. How did the Giants accomplish all this?

They knew, somewhere inside each player, and collectively as a team, they could win. It is what the Europeans did in the 2012 Ryder Cup. They never stopped believing they could win. They became a force that was, on some level, unstoppable. Such a force is what makes human beings unique among species that have ever inhabited this Earth. Call it soul. Call it spirit. Call it faith. Call it feeling. Call it light in the darkness. An eternal flame. Or call it by a name that is unnamable. It is not knowable. It is not religion. It is not something that can be learned, nor studied, nor rehearsed. It is something of the breath, something inspired, something arising from the core of being. Something inexplicable.

And when the Giants entered the World Series, that force, that inner sound, had grown to such a crescendo, the Tigers didn't know what hit them. Pablo Sandoval was the first to sound the trumpet. Homer in the first. Homer in the third. Homer in the fifth. Like Tiger Woods in the year 2000. Boom. Boom. Boom. The other team, the other competitors, were numb. The word "competitor" was an oxymoron. It was no longer a relevant word, and in those moments it could have justifiably been struck from the lexicon, replaced by the word "intimidation," or some other word not yet evolved that could carry even more force. Something like intimadegradation. Or grindimolation. Or grundched. That's it: Sandoval grundched Detroit. They became a team of zombies walking around with heads near their knees and shoulders hunched like potatoes.

What's remarkable is just a few weeks before, the Giants looked just as grundched. They could have easily folded and packed up and pulled up stakes for this season and unboarded up their beach houses for the winter. It would have been entirely human to call it quits, to throw in the towel, to follow a final beer with a bump down the road, and get their hearts out of San Francisco. But they didn't. No, they sure as hell didn't. They hung in there. They toughed it out. They dug in. They came back. Just like Keegan did at the PGA. And Rory did after blowing the Masters. And Padraig did after double bogeying at the Open. And Ernie did dropping that 15-footer at the British. You never say die. You pick yourself up by the bootstraps. You grit your teeth. You bite the bullet. You *giter done*. You find a way. You hitch up your pants. You rip off your shirt, get on your knees, and shout, "YES!" like Brandi Chastain did at the World Cup in '99 after beating China on a penalty kick.

In golf in 2012, we saw a year of the comeback, capped off by Tommy "Two Gloves" Gainey, former South Carolina factory worker, come from seven back to win his first PGA tournament. He did that by swinging 100 percent on every one of his sixty strokes on the final day. His mind was focused not on winning but on remaining committed and focused on every shot he took on that day. Like the Giants, he kept a tight rein on his potentially runaway mind, galloping away with thoughts of "What if I win?" and "What will I say at the award presentation?" and "How will I spend all that money?"

No, he pegged his ball on each hole, already forgetting what he did on the last hole and concentrated on hitting the ball on the screws, on the sweet spot, on making a good swing, on choosing the right club. Just like the Giants who were down 3-1 against the Reds and devoted not a neuron to negative thoughts, "Two Gloves" stayed in the moment throughout the game, doing what he's trained to do, thinking not of what the opposing players would do, knowing what he was capable of doing, and performing shot by shot by shot.

Golf and baseball are alike in that way. You can have an awful front nine, pounding yourself into oblivion, ready to call the fight, bloodied against the ropes, and, Bingo, you eagle the 10th like Rory McIlroy did at the 2014 PGA. Then you par the 11th and 12th, and "Great God in Heaven" you birdie the 13th. Suddenly, miraculously, as if angels were dancing in the cavity backs of your irons, you're back in the game, looking at the possibility of breaking 90 or 80, or whatever it is you're trying to break. Or you win the PGA after an awful front nine like Rory. And, like baseball, it's a slow enough game where the contrast of such a miracle is enough to shock you with the power of the present moment. For once you let go of the reality of the debacles of the front nine, or, in the Giants case, the entire first half of the season, you release yourself of the burden of those fiascos. Like the monkey who can open his fist, release the food, and escape from the gourd trap, you are free of all hindrances, and can fulfill your potential. In a flash, you are an enlightened athlete, in the moment, fully awake, and alive to life.

Do you see how we can apply this to our lives? Regardless of the adversity, we go forward. We resist the temptation to look back and turn ourselves to salt. There's no room for doubt as we apply the fundamentals that we've learned and concentrate on the basics of solid contact with the present moment, of hitting that 7-iron hard and true, of eyeing that fastball coming in at the knees, of timing that head shot with the flight of the ball from the corner, of nailing that interview for that job you've been hoping for, of remembering to buy those flowers for your favorite squeeze, of coming back after an horrendous hurricane.

The Giants, with true grit, taught us all that.

HOLE 5
Learning

YOU CAN TAKE up golf at any age, and sometimes the older the better. Too often the young player gets into bad habits, spending years trying to get out of them. In my own case, I got very good at an early age, then life happened and I left the game, losing many of my skills, then spent years steeped in frustration trying to return to excellence. Again, the mind and your approach to the game are key.

The Measured Swing

There are many moving parts to a golf swing, and the arms, being integral to most swings in most sports, are among the most important. In golf, it's the forward arm (left for the right-hander, right for the left-hander) that is critical. It, and its elbow, must be kept straight through most of the swing, about three quarters of it. The golf club, of course, is pre-measured. You can grip down on it, affecting its length, but its length is set once the swing has begun. The arm, with its elbow, bends naturally, and that presents a particular challenge. In order to maintain a swing that is consistent and measured, the forward arm must be kept straight during a swing that is moving the club anywhere from 70 to 120 mph. In no other sport is this required. This

is usually not a problem at the very beginning of the backswing. But there reaches a point in the swing when most golfers get a bit greedy and want to overextend the backswing, get a little more distance in an effort to really give it a crack this time, to really get out there with the big hitters, to reach that 150-yard marker so they'll have a chance to hit the green in regulation . . . this time. So they try to turn the shoulders just a bit more, and in the process, depending on their degree of flexibility, bend the forward arm at the top of the backswing.

Once the integrity of that arm is violated, things get chaotic. You could recover and make good contact, but more likely it's a game of Russian roulette. Where the swing path and clubhead go from there is like a car on the freeway with a blown tire. What's likely is what is called "hitting from the top." To compensate for the bent arm, the hands and wrists flail about and break too soon, often sweeping the club across the ball from outside the swing plane to inside after impact, imparting a clockwise spin on the ball, producing the dreaded, though very common, slice to the extreme right for a right-hander. This, in turn, produces some equally common curse words universal throughout the golf world. We've even given this aberration a special identifying tag: "the chicken wing."

So the fix is to limit the backswing to where the forward arm remains straight, and go no further. In other words, keep the integrity of a straight arm. This then sets up a downswing where the lag between the wrist and arm can lead to a very powerful impact position. But if the arm breaks down, so will the lag, most of the time. For examples, think Chi Chi Rodriguez, Doug Sanders, and presently, Jason Dufner, Robert Allenby, and Tommy "Two Gloves" Gainey. Their backswings are relatively short, keeping the integrity of that forward arm until well after impact. It's a great swing thought to rely upon since it's simple and direct and easy to achieve. It concentrates the attention onto the forward elbow, encouraging full extension of the arm through impact. The tricky part is getting the timing right between the backswing and the beginning of the downswing. You'll need to work that out on the range. In another chapter, I recommend using the forward shoulder hitting the chin as the key move and cue to starting the downswing.

By the way, this straight, forward arm fix isn't just a figment of my particular mammalian brain. Ben Hogan wrote of the importance of this swing tenet in *Five Lessons: The Modern Fundamentals of Golf.* "The left arm, straight at address, remains straight throughout the backswing while the right folds in at the elbow. On the downswing, the left continues to be fully extended and the right gradually straightens out."

Without this measured swing, it's likely that no divot will be taken with an iron, denying the club its ability to get the ball airborne with enough spin to hold the green.

Ah yes, the divot. I once attempted a full 9-iron as a boy in my living room and took a divot in the rug, hiding it from my mother by sewing it back together with heavy-duty thread. I think I was fifty and she was eighty before I told her, and had a good laugh about it. We get the message early on that we shouldn't put holes in pretty things where no holes are intended. And so when we're told to replace divots on a golf course, our minds go back to childhood, telling us we're really not supposed to make divots. We soon find that bending the forward arm will effectively let us scoop the ball off the turf without even a scuff to the lovely grass. The problem gets compounded when beginners see that more seasoned golfers often don't replace their divots anyway, making the place look like the surface of the moon. All they have to do is keep that forward arm bent and the untidy problem doesn't even get started.

There are other elements of the measured swing that also must be addressed. The head has to be relatively still. It can move slightly horizontally, but it must be kept still vertically. Why? Because this keeps you in the same relative distance to the ball throughout the swing. How to keep the head still is a function of the eyes. Watch the back of the ball particularly as the downswing starts, for it's here that the head is in most danger of moving vertically, making it more likely to lower the plane of the body and hit the shot fat.

Finally, a crucial hinge of the body involves the hips and spine. A measured swing must be kept on the same plane throughout, but the tendency is to come out of the plane as the golfer approaches impact. It's not easy to "stay with it" as you swing a forty-five-inch driver ninety mph. It's not something our bodies were meant to do. But do it we must if we are to keep the swing measured. So pick an initial plane that is comfortable for your height and body type, and stick with it as you swing through impact. Keeping the eyes fixed on the ball through impact will help keep you "on plane."

So your swing is now measured but is it properly timed and in sync? Probably not, if you're like me and don't have much time to play. Every time I venture out to the links, I need to warm up on the range to see what particular timing and rhythm I bring to the course that day. I hate tee times because they often make me rush through this initial practice period. What I start with, though, is a straight, forward arm, even building that into my forward press. In other words, at address, my left arm is straight yet relaxed. To trigger the swing, my forward press stiffens the arm slightly, a signal to begin the backswing. That arm then remains straight and relatively stiff through impact. Watch videos of Jack in his prime or Rory now to see examples of what I'm referring to.

However, as an old Buddhist teacher of mine, Ajahn Sumedho, used to tell us, after presenting his lecture, "But don't just listen to me: Go out and try it for yourself."

The Key Move

The key move in the execution of a golf swing turns out to be a simple one indeed. I don't know why it's not emphasized more. I've taken a number of lessons over my sixty years in the game, and it was never mentioned once. Not even hinted at. People always asked Hogan what was his secret, and he always replied "It's in the dirt," implying that a great deal of practice was the answer. But that assumes you are practicing the proper fundamentals. Most golfers often do not. The move is a subtle one. You will barely notice it, and no one else will see it happening. That's the catch and probably why it was never pointed out to me before. You can feel the move, but you can't see it. Well, you can *see* it, but it takes very close observation. I discovered this move after hearing a chance remark about it by Gary McCord on a golf telecast. Yes, Gary McCord, the funny guy with the handlebar stash who has won a total of two professional tournaments, both on the Champions Tour. The man, though, knows the golf swing. I've seen him play, and he hits the ball a country mile. Here's what Gary had to say, addressed to a right-handed golfer: "Keep your left arm near your chest and swing them (your chest and your arm) at the same pace, keeping your arm connected to your chest."

Now we don't often think of keeping our arm connected to our chest, but what that does is unify a part of our body that, for a golf swing, needs unifying. Separating them is like separating the drive train from the engine of a car: it doesn't go very far or fast. When you connect them in this fashion, you feel as if the entire body is behind the swing, generating power. The ball is the recipient of that power, and it is designed to take it full on. Of course there are other fundamentals required to make sure the ball travels in the intended line and trajectory of flight. Things like a steady head, a measured left arm, turning (not swaying) hips, and about a million other items, as Rocco might say. But the foot or so from the time you drag the club away from the address position to before you lift it to the top of the backswing is "the key move." It is the heart and soul of the one-piece takeaway. Mining it deeper in search of the cell of that takeaway is the connection between the forward arm (left in the right-hander, right in the left-hander) and its relationship with the chest that is the absolute core.

For golf is a matter of relationship, with your body, your mind, your emotions, your environment, your playing partners, the golf course, your consciousness, and your ability to bounce back from disappointment and despair. When you enter the arena of the golf course (or even driving range, for that matter), you enter a kind of coliseum, rife with lions and spectators out for your blood. These of course are mental constructs, reflective of the characters parading about in your own mind, but the course is not only a place of fun and relaxation but also a place of high drama. And you'd better have your proverbial shit together if you want to come out of the experience with any modicum of self-respect and pride. And where to start is the foot or eighteen inches, which start the takeaway on the backswing.

Ironically, to practice this key move, you don't need a golf course, a driving range, golf clubs, or a ball. A full-length mirror would be nice, but you even don't really need that. You need to stand up, take your address position, hold an imaginary club, and begin your swing, and do this over and over. You can do the move in the bathroom before your shower, in your cubicle at work, waiting for the commuter train, in an elevator; hell, you can do it while you're in the shower. As I said above, you can't really see this move. You feel it, and feel it you must. The hands, arms, shoulders, legs, and chest work as a unit, the true one-piece takeaway, and the weight begins to shift to the inside of the right foot, which keeps you from swaying your hips. The left arm remains relatively, not rigidly, straight, and moves in direct relation to the chest, at the same pace, as McCord says. The hands do not operate independently, *in any way.* They simply hold the club properly and are part of the drive train for the engine of the core/chest. They work in unison as the club begins its ascent to the top of the backswing. Think Steve Stricker, Lee Janzen, and Robert Allenby, all of whose swings can be seen on YouTube.

As a car engine will sputter and falter and fail if the pace of the pistons is not consistent, and so will the golf swing. The overriding element is pace. For every club in the bag it must be the same. I like to imagine and practice a seven-iron pace for every club, including the driver, which is the toughest club in the bag to hit because it's the toughest seven-iron pace to maintain. Sometimes, I'll go back in memory and picture and apply my "Gene Littler" pace to each swing. Or sometimes, my "Ernie Els" pace, or my "Sam Snead" or "Bobby Jones" pace. These images or mental suggestions are very important, since pace is so easy to forget during the course of a round. The amateur can be quite affected by the pace of others who are hitting the ball farther. The mind can link on to the pace of others and very subtly change your pace without you knowing it. It doesn't take much to knock the golf swing off balance and off rhythm.

But the place to start is at the start of the backswing, along with the image of Gene Littler (they called him "Gene the Machine" back in the sixties, and you can conjure him up on YouTube to see what I mean), or whoever your pace idol happens to be. Then move the chest and left arm as a unit, and a lot of the rest of what happens is a function of gravity.

The Key Downswing Move

At the transition between the back and downswings there is a point in time and space that sets the tone for the coup de grace of the golf swing, namely impact—that vital moment when the hands lead the clubhead down and into the ball, compressing the ball like a trampoline, firing with a mortar shell's trajectory, tracing an elliptical surge. The battlefield of golf. An explosion of energy, an expression of aggression, a rifle's recoil. We shop at the market. We drive in traffic. We work at ordinary jobs in ordinary buildings with ordinary people who wish us ordinary good mornings, good nights, and good weekends. All pretty low-key stuff. But the impact zone of a golf swing? That's bombastic. That's hyperbolic. That's sesquipedalian. I don't care if you're Betty White swinging at sixty mph: the impact zone of a golf swing is exciting.

I know most instructors teach that the downswing starts with the legs and hips, followed by the upper body and arms, but I have a different take on it. Watch any slo-mo Peter Kostis analysis of a pro's swing, and you'll see that the downswing starts with the hands and arms moving almost in unison with the lower body into the impact zone. The pros, with their hours of practice, can gain some extra yards with the hips and legs generating more clubhead speed, but it's much harder for handicappers to get the sequence right. The consequence is often a shot that is off-line or hit fat or thin, none of which will feel satisfying. In fact, I recommend higher handicap amateurs only pay attention to the arms during the swing. The lower body will take care of itself. It's a swing, after all, and, for most, a swing involves the arms primarily. The advantage to this is that there's less to think about during the swing, and that you will hit the ball more squarely in the center of your iron or wood. With today's clubs that means enough distance to get the job done, and enough accuracy to keep the ball in play.

Simply have your weight about 60 percent on your forward foot at address for irons, and 60 percent on your rear foot for woods (hybrids should be treated as irons), and, after the key backswing moves, initiate the downswing by pulling the butt of the forward hand downward toward the ball. That key downswing move is the signal for the body to begin moving more of its weight forward and clearing the hips out of the way to allow the arms and hands to swing through. But most importantly, this move delays the hit, creating a greater angle of lag between the wrists and the arms. This delay, when approaching the impact area, is the harbinger of power.

So, after setting your weight up properly, the swing thought/action is simply to pull the butt of the club downward toward the ball at a pace about the same as you would for your 7-iron for all clubs. Your grip should, of course, be in your fingers, allowing the free movement of the hands and wrists in the downswing. As evolution has dictated, your mind expects the hands and arms to be in control of any swinging motion. Witness any chimpanzee. The nerve endings there are conditioned to react to an implement, in this case the golf club, that needs to be swung to fulfill its function, in this case propelling a golf ball a long way, accurately. Fingers are designed for fine, detailed work like gripping, holding, and directing. The grosser body will follow the fingers. And the move conveniently and automatically tucks the right elbow into the right side of the body where it should be at the early stages of the downswing. One less thing to think about in this complicated series of movements called the golf swing.

From the top of the backswing, there is a forward inertia that moves the entire body into the impact zone, with one exception: the head doesn't move. With the forward foot firmly planted, the left side stiffens at impact, allowing you to "hit against a firm left side." Braced as such, the hands and wrists can release and whip the clubhead squarely into the ball.

The longer the club, the wider the stance, providing more of a base to control the swing. This will depend on your height though, as well. With all this swinging, golf truly is a balance sport and a hand-eye coordination sport. The keystone in the above instruction is the head. With any head movement, there is a risk you will lose accuracy. Tiger Woods used to dip his head at the start of the downswing, and his driving would, and still does, get him into trouble. When two-time U.S. Open champ Retief Goosen was a kid learning the game in South Africa, his teacher would literally hold his head in place as he swung, to teach him what that felt like and how it could affect the results. The head is the axle. The hands and arms are the spokes. The body is the chassis.

You can apply this key move to almost any club in the bag. Just position the ball more toward the middle of the stance, the shorter the club. It works for the driver down to the wedges. Putting is a game unto itself. Entire books have been written on it alone.

And, of course, there is the mind. I tried out my key downswing move a few years ago, had great success on the range, then flopped with it on the course the first time out. As often happens, I tried modifying the technique as I was playing and wound up getting into deeper and deeper trouble. The mind was looking for a way out of its misery. So instead of sticking with the method and letting it find its level during actual play, I grew impatient and started my infernal trial and error routine, which is a recipe for disaster when you're playing. When the pros talk about "staying patient," I think this is what they're talking about. Stay with the swing thoughts and actions you last practiced on the range and don't change them because of a few bad shots.

This technique of driving the butt of the forward hand down toward the ball on the downswing may take a while to settle into the mind and body. You may hit a few fat shots until the body finds the right timing in its move forward (the key here is to practice the weight shift advice at address). But practice it on the range for a while. Get comfortable with it. Let your confidence grow so you begin to expect positive results. Then take it to the course and see if it holds up. If it does, great. Ride the wave. If it doesn't, that's OK too. Return to the range and make sure you've ingrained the technique into your routine. It's all grist for the game improvement mill.

Of course, I'm aware of the naysayers and Hoganistas who claim that the downswing is a sequence of movements starting from the legs up. That's valid for pros. But I see the swing as two units: the backswing, starting with the key move and keeping the core connected with the arms; and the downswing, initiated by pulling the club down with the hands, leading the arms, hips, and legs toward impact together. The average golfer cannot master the precise synchronizations required of Hogan's techniques. There's just too much to remember and to put into the right order. And there's just too little time to practice these moves, particularly as the body ages and social obligations intercede. My method does not need as much practice, brings the entire body into the equation without worrying so much about timing, and is generally easier on the hips, knees, and back, something to consider if any of those is a problem. If golf is easier to learn and play, more people will come to and stay with the game. But don't take my word as gospel: try it and find out for yourself.

Impact

I was at a driving range and watching people, as I often do, negotiating the impact position of the golf swing. For a beginner, impact is a daunting prospect. Holding a club (the very sound of which is cumbersome and cavemanlike), they are expected to strike this fairly small, dimpled, very solid ball, which is farther away from the body and the eye than in any other ball and bat sport. And they are instructed to strike the iron clubs down on the ball to make it go up. Pretty weird when you stop to think of it. And for fastidious people, the thought of taking a divot from this beautiful turf is against everything their mothers taught them. So beginners will try to scoop the ball off the turf by crooking their forward arm at impact, so as not to damage the ground.

I've seen this over and over, no matter how lousy the results. Or the head will pull up too soon, trying to peek at where the ball went even before it gets there. Backswings can look fine. Good positions, proper weight shift. Club in an OK position at the top. But then the downswing commences and all hell breaks loose. Weight can stay on the back foot. Lag is spent early. Wrists break too soon, causing the club to come over the top, with the clubhead pointing left, causing a pull or slice. Head is . . . well, let's just say it's not where it's supposed to be.

Why does all this happen? The dreaded anticipation of impact. It's where golf suddenly becomes a high-action sport. Up there with a baseball pitch. A football dive over the line. A basketball slam dunk. A cricket whatever. An ice hockey goal. A soccer header goal. It's where the blur happens. The blur is the action that needs the slo-mo camera to see what's happening. The blur is a bit shocking, unexpected, chaotic, out of control, if only for a moment in time. It needs the expert's analysis of the mechanics behind it all. It's the action you know just happened but don't exactly know how you got there, or how to remedy it if it goes awry. Bobby Clampett wrote an entire book on this, called *The Impact Zone*. Master instructor Sean Foley, who coaches several touring pros, advises setting up a half-dozen balls and swinging at each one from 10 percent of max to 90 percent in 20 percent increments to feel what impact feels like at different paces. Davis Love III says swing in super slow motion to break down impact into its lowest common denominators.

All of us, even many touring pros, dread impact. They are so sure of pre-shot routines, set up, takeaway, backswing, start of downswing, but after the downswing starts and impact approaches, even the great

Phil Mickelson is looking at a crapshoot. For just the slightest miscue, the slightest change in pace or rhythm, the most minor change in timing, can affect the position of the clubface at impact. And that affects how and where the ball will fly.

So what chance do we golfing mortals have at impact? If you're like me, you don't play this game enough to get really good at it. So you have to have a strategy that fits your game and the amount of time you have to play or practice. One of the problems at impact is that the hands and wrists turn over too quickly as they move toward the follow through. Now the hands and wrists do indeed turn over, or pronate, as the follow through progresses, but not until they pass impact. At impact, for a right-hander, the right hand remains behind the left as both hands, combined, deliver the coup de grace. The hips have already done their job. Now the hands and arms are moving as fast as a stock car on a straightaway.

So what I do is make sure that the right hand doesn't overtake the left too soon (this can also be depicted as the right forearm overtaking the left forearm), something my instructor calls "holding off that inevitable pronation move." Of course, you can overdo this, resulting in a push or slice, so practice: a lot of practice is needed to nail this move. My swing thought here is to think of the right hand staying behind the left at impact. I do this to break my conditioning over the years to pronate too soon. I know I do this since my misses are mostly to the left, either pulls, hooks, or a combination of the two. Pronation will close the clubface, causing a right to left spin.

Phil suffered a spell of this during the second round of the Deutsche Bank Championship during the 2013 FedEx Playoffs. For four or five holes on the back nine, "Lefty" mostly hooked his tee ball far right into the dense trees. With the replay slo-mo, you could see how his left hand started pronating at impact instead of holding off some. Most of these went right, and one or two went left. Russian roulette golf. Of course, Phil being Phil, he hit a couple of the most amazing recovery shots I've ever seen, particularly an explosion from a cuppy, near-impossible lie near the green to get up and down for par.

But you could see how frustrated he was with his long game for that stretch. For us golfing mortals, it could ruin a round. He finished the round with two birds and was well in contention. So you can bet he figured something out.

Of course, proper alignment is critical as well. If you're aligned too far to the right of target, the tendency is to commit the hands and wrists too early, producing an over the top move or a premature pronation at impact. The former will produce a slice, and the latter a hook. Misalignment sends a false message from the mind to the body for the need to compensate, setting up the swing for a clubface that is not square at impact. And your goal as a golfer is to come into impact with a clubface square to the target.

This last thought is important to remember. For when we stand up to any given shot, no matter how easy or difficult we perceive it to be, our goal, after aligning our body properly, is to make a good swing. Then we have a better chance of staying in the present moment with this game. That's the challenge. For if we are always thinking about our potential score, or where we want to place the shot, or the consequences if we don't hit the next shot well, or the pond to the right of the green, we are immediately out of the present moment and into the future. You can't play good golf in the future. It's a game that must be played with as few mental distractions as possible. And that means staying present with the movements of our body.

The point of impact, which Bobby Clampett calls "the moment of truth," is happening so fast that the body must be unencumbered of thoughts around potential results. Keep that in mind, then let it go, then swing away. And if at first you don't succeed, try, try again, à la Phil Mickelson.

HOLE 6
Improving

GOLFERS, AS A species, love the feel of a well-struck golf shot—a sensation that perhaps comes closest to the experience of enlightenment, without the esoteric austerities of hours on the cushion and endless interviews with meditation teachers. Of course, hard work and commitment are still required to attain that kind of blissful present-ness. And once you've tasted the oneness of solid contact with the ball, you will strive to improve so you can dip into golf mindfulness again and again.

Concentration forms the keystone of the arch that the golfer walks beneath. Once you're present and at peace with that stationary ball before you, improvement can follow.

The Challenge of Concentration

As we see from the playing of any PGA tournament, golf requires sustained and all-encompassing concentration on every shot. This is a daunting task that most golfers often back down from. I remember during a three-month meditation retreat at the Insight Meditation Society (IMS) in Barre, Massachusetts, many years ago, I reached a point of realization that every moment required an absolute state of

presentness of mind. This thought overwhelmed me and I had to take a break from the retreat to reflect upon such an awesome insight. A depression overcame me, and I became dispirited and even demoralized. It was too much to handle. Every moment, even the most mundane, required me to be present and aware. Finally, I realized there was no way to escape this reality and, after a struggle, I settled into whatever the present moment dealt me. So I began to notice even the turning of a door handle, the lifting of a fork, the separate chews that led to the swallowing of each bite of food, each step from my room to the dining hall, and, of course, each breath in the meditation hall. Eventually, I reached a state of deep samadhi, or concentration. I was the happiest I'd ever been, my only accomplishment being heightened attention to the mundane. To this day, I can still remember individual bites of food I took during that retreat.

This state of mind and body, though, did not stay with me without effort. Each moment required a renewal of my resolve to pay attention, to not venture beyond the present to anticipate what might happen in the moment ahead. We humans spend inordinate amounts of time in the future or the past, and so miss out on the gifts of the present: the presents of the present, so to speak. As I settled into the present at that retreat, my patience with the present grew until I didn't have to devote as much time reminding myself to "Be Here Now," as Ram Dass once reminded all of us back in the Sixties. The present folded into my consciousness more naturally, and I found a great peace of mind attending to the mundane events of daily life.

Of course, golf represents a great training ground for the practice of staying present. We even have a score to quantify our efforts. And, in the competition ranks, we have a winner who is able to best stay in the moments of the intense fray, especially at the finish when the heat is highest, especially during professional majors. Ask Phil when he overcooked a wedge to lose the '13 U.S. Open, where his mind was at the time. Ask Lee Westwood when he repeatedly missed three-footers to lose several majors that he had in his grasp. And ask Tiger when he dropped a twelve-footer on the 72nd hole at Torrey Pines to tie Rocco Mediate in '08 and go on to win, where he was in relation to the present at the time.

Concentration, then, is remaining present, no matter what the content of that present moment is. As renowned meditation teacher and author Jack Kornfield says often, "Every moment is no more or less important than every other moment." That is an extremely profound statement, which can be applied to anything in life. Golf is one area of life where you can see the results of your efforts at such concentration more graphically than most other areas where results often take months or years to unfold. In golf, the spoils of concentration are visible after one shot, adding up to a good score or dejection.

The problem in golf, as in life, is that we are conditioned to be anticipating what's ahead. We are strategizing constantly, planning where to place the next shot to set up the subsequent shot, or how hard to hit a putt so as not to go too far past the hole and face a knee-knocker coming back, or fearing a water hazard off the tee and what that might do to our score if we land in it. Now, given the nature of this sport and all its variables, we do have to anticipate and plan ahead, but the challenge is to do this planning before we swing. Once we address the ball and we know where we want to aim, we need to concentrate on the fundamentals which we've learned will lead to as good an effort as we can make to reach the target we've picked. Annika Sorenstam talks about a box she stands in behind the ball, assessing and thinking through her shot, before addressing the ball. Once she takes her stance, all thoughts of assessment are over. Step by step, she takes her stance, places her hands in the proper grip position, aligns her body properly, has a swing thought or two, takes a waggle of sorts, and pulls the trigger. This is the essence of concentration, and Annika's record shows what such effort can bring.

For weekend dubs and more advanced amateurs the procedure to enter into the present is the same. Of course, we have the added burden, at times, of conversation that spills over onto the tee box. One buddy of mine, once he gets started on a hot subject, can't seem to stop even as he assumes his address position. He'll even walk away to finish his point, until he finally realizes that "While we're young," moment when he sees that he's holding up play. If I get caught up in his monologue about a Supreme Court ruling or some political idiocy coming out of Congress, I'm doomed before I even start my pre-shot routine. So I have extra work involved in clearing my mind of whatever verbal spillover I'm hearing, and use my meditation skills to return to the quiet present and the golf shot at hand.

And the present *is* a wonderfully quiet space. It's one of the great pleasures of meditation to hang out in that quiet, given the cacophony of our usual everyday lives. The golf course is one of those quieter places that gives us respite from the noise of the street, and so the practice of concentration is easier there than it is on the street or the road or at work.

When I did that meditation retreat years ago, there was a banner at IMS that simply said, "Remember." This is one of the keys of concentration while playing golf. You have to continually remind yourself to remember to enlist all your strategies for staying present, and to consciously oppose any obstacles to that hallowed state of mind. Have your conversations about this or that between shots, but when it's time to play your shot, enter into another zone of being: a quiet, clear, fresh, alive, conscious, sensitive, wise, confident, calm, happy zone where the busy, noisy world is no more. It's just you; your mind and body, ready to give that golf ball a smooth and present ride into history.

Owning your Swing

Watching the Accenture Match Play tournament a while ago, I was struck with one of the essential elements of golf: competition. Whether you're playing in a friendly weekend foursome or the Masters, golfers want to beat other golfers. Even if you're playing alone, you want to beat the course or the diabolical architect who designed it or your best score. I'm not talking final score either, although in a club, junior, or USGA tournament, that's important; I'm talking about individual drives, approach shots, chips, bunker shots, and putts. We want to outdo each other. I won't show it, but down under the skin, I'm annoyed when my seventy-six-year-old golf buddy, Steve, outdrives me, and when he birdies a hole to my bogey, I'll congratulate him, but I'm not at all happy for him. I know this is quite un-Buddhist of me as Buddhists eschew competition and envy, but it must be part of my genetic makeup. My dad was a pretty decent amateur boxer, and my brother Hank played ball just behind Wilt Chamberlain at Overbrook High in Philly.

In fact, I don't even like it when someone out-meditates me. I want to be the best student, lasting the longest (made it to seventeen continuous hours once on a retreat), and being the most equanimous. I come across as being a mellow fellow, but down deep, I want to prevail in competitive situations. In meditation, it's not cool to admit this, although I've observed this competitive tendency in other practitioners, particularly in touting their meditative cred. But in golf, it's prevalent in most players I've observed, regardless of gender.

To embrace this element of competitiveness adds an edge to the game that for amateurs gives a taste of what the pros experience. Competition is the reason most of us can't take our progress at the range to the course. It translates into pressure, which translates into tension, which translates into a fat 7-iron that came out of nowhere. But competition and the pressure that follows are also what make us want to improve.

The best antidote for pressure that arises out of competition is to own your swing. Tiger was asked about this, whether he owned his swing as Hogan did. Typical Woods, he said it was a work in progress, but that he was getting closer. He was talking about a major swing overhaul, the umpteenth since turning pro. Why did Woods need another overhaul? The answer I think is that pressure and competition, over time, will wear down the gears of a well-tuned swing. Bobby Jones discovered this to be true, and retired from competitive golf at twenty-eight after he won the Grand Slam. The swing is such a nuanced action that it is affected by even the slightest changes wrought by the ravages of age and pressure. If you battle or ignore or deny the changes, you will surely lose. You have to adapt, to modify, to think through and experiment with the changes that are needed. Tiger has said that he is able to make a fix quickly after a mis-hit, and that may be the main factor between an amateur and a pro of his caliber. Even though he is often revamping it, Tiger, perhaps less now than in his prime, owns his swing.

After each round, you should be able to have an increasing sense of swing ownership. The course is the real testing grounds, because that's where the pressure is. The range is Easy Acres. No pressure whatsoever. For ownership, every gain on the range needs to be subjected to the rigors of the course. Keeping score is critical since to not do so eliminates, for all intents and purposes, pressure. There is certainly a time for not keeping score, namely a practice round, but pressure is what adds that reality-show edge to your game. Of course you can choose to make golf a stroll in the park (and from my perspective, that's perfectly OK), but to risk making it "a good walk spoiled," and play with the edges of disaster, you have to keep score.

Because at those edges are the opportunities to learn and improve. "Every adversity has within it the seed of an equal or greater benefit," wrote Napoleon Hill, and keeping score, along with competition, guarantees golf will offer many adversities to dig for those benefits. So your score is a means to an end of constant improvement. Unfortunately, most golfers consider the score the end all, be all, and miss the chance for deeper ownership of their swing, within which lies the true satisfaction of this game. Breaking 90 or 80 may be something you'll remember and be proud of for a long time, but the more you own your swing, the deeper the satisfaction every time you swing the club. In meditation, such ownership of one's very being—what Buddhists call the True Self—translates into tremendous freedom and happiness.

I submit that the reason we play golf is to experience that kind of freedom of the body and happiness of the spirit and soul. Whether you're twenty-five or ninety, you can get both from a well-executed golf swing. The score is not so much a measure of your proficiency but of how much you own your swing and your own mind. And, as in life, the way to deepen that ownership is to approach the game as a true student and never stop learning. Complete ownership of our body, our mind, and our golf swing is called enlightenment, which can only be attained through the practice of a spiritual warrior, or one who wakes up each day, puts feet firmly on the ground, and fearlessly says, "What can I learn today?"

Golf is a Game of Balance

Golf involves such an intricate array of muscle movements that if you are out of balance just slightly, the flight of the ball will be affected negatively. Being a student of meditation and a teacher of Tai Chi, I have observed how a loss of balance can catapult you out the present moment and into a precarious flirtation with chaos. In golf, that chaos translates as mis-hit shots, poor decisions around course management, and letting big numbers affect your entire day. In life, losing one's balance can be much more catastrophic, like the sad case of three hikers in Yosemite who waded into a pool above Vernal Fall, slipping, and going over the edge to their deaths. Other examples include elderly people who land in nursing homes because of a fall, and those who lose their emotional balance, resulting in serious psychological disorders. With golf, the effects of imbalance are not as dramatic as I've just described—it's a game, after all—but if you're serious about golf, it can be no less frustrating and aggravating when your game goes awry.

As I've mentioned before, Tiger Woods—one of the greatest golfers in the modern era—is an example of how someone who was so successful for almost ten years could fall so grossly out of balance on physical, emotional, and spiritual levels in such a short period of time. At his lowest point, he was a prime role model of how not to live life. It shows how balance is such a fragile and fickle state. We have billions of nerve cells in the human body. Those cells are such that a paper cut or a pebble in your shoe or a bitten lip can draw your attention and knock you off balance for any number of moments or hours. Even mellow Rory McIlroy lost his balance early in his career by telling a commentator and former pro, via Twitter, to "Shut up! You're just a commentator and failed pro. Your opinions mean nothing . . . "

So how to insure that we remain in or return to balance when we swing a golf club? First, if you are physically out of balance, take time to let the body rest and recuperate, and seek medical treatment when necessary. It seems like simple, common sense advice but too many ignore what the body is trying to tell them. Denial is not a treatment option. You observe and listen to the body, then take a proactive, reasonable, and rational approach toward healing. I hit a rock in a bunker a few years ago, ignored the pain in my elbow, and wound up having to take a year off from the game. If I'd acted sooner, that healing time might have been shortened. Once, pro Mike Weir had to withdraw from the Canadian Open—his home country's national Open—because of an elbow injury exacerbated when hitting out of deep rough. Like me, Weir had golfer's elbow. And like me, Weir was in denial about it. He needed an extended rest to let that elbow heal. And, as I've discovered, it will heal.

Emotional imbalance is often more difficult to confront and keep from affecting your game. If you are continually thinking about the fight you just had with your spouse, or the credit card debt you're in, or the account you just lost at work, those worries will hit your swing like a howitzer. Don't believe me? See how you finish your swing. Are you in balance or practically falling over backward? And where did the ball go? Left, right; left, right? Skittering along the ground like a prairie dog diving for cover? It's tough to get those proper swing elements humming when you're obsessing over something that's troubling you. You're coming to the course to get away from all that trouble, but you still bring it with you in your own mind. So the answer lies within your own mind. And that's the good news. You may not be able to change the trouble but you can affect your relationship to it. And when you're playing golf, your relationship to anything other than playing golf in that moment is to distance yourself from it. It's a kind of creative, conscious repression of the trouble. You can't do anything about it, so put it aside while you are devoting your full energy to playing golf. Before you start playing, you can have a plan for how you'll deal with your problems, like therapy, or hiring a financial advisor or life coach, or reading a good self-help book, or attending a self development workshop or consulting your minister or rabbi or Zen master or imam or guru or medicine man. There are any number of positive actions you can take to solve emotional problems. But the golf course is not the place to figure them out. It's the place to chill out.

Now the last level of imbalance is spiritual, perhaps the thorniest of all. For if you are embroiled in a midlife crisis or a lapse of faith or wondering what life is all about or just getting older and losing your life purpose, it's difficult to stay in the moment as golf requires. These are existential issues, and poor golf performance will only deepen the dilemmas. A vicious cycle ensues; and before you know it, you're thinking of giving up the game. I recently read Kris Tschetter's excellent book, *Mr. Hogan: The Man I Knew,* and I believe Ben Hogan went through this in his final years, according to Tschetter's account of her unusual friendship with the great man. Increasingly, Hogan lost interest in playing the game, partly because of leg and hip pain, I'm sure, but partly because he lost his purpose in life (with the exception of coaching LPGA pro Tschetter), with the sale of his golf club business and subsequent decrease in quality of his clubs, and gradual loss of those few friends he'd been close to. He eventually developed dementia and increasingly lost touch with the world. Hogan was unable to adapt to the changing conditions of life, as Jones, Nelson, Player, Nicklaus, and Palmer were able to do. Preventing a crisis in spirit involves flexibility, keeping active, modifying your life purpose as the body ages, and having a strong social network. A spiritual practice like meditation helps, along with contact with a sangha, or community of like-minded practitioners. Your Saturday morning foursome just won't do it, I'm afraid, unless it's with friends from the Shivas Irons Society, a group of admirers of Michael Murphy's spiritual golf book, *Golf in the Kingdom.*

Feeling balanced, you can swing the club freely, without hindrance or restrictions or thoughts that skulk about like characters in a bad dream. This is not to say you won't screw up a round from time to time, but you will feel better when you finish a shot in balance or hit a putt solidly or nail a wedge from 100 yards. Then you can see your game in perspective: a game that helps you stay present and enjoy your life to the fullest as the moments unfold.

The Athletic Golf Swing

The athletic golf swing has been demonstrated by a number of greats throughout golfing history. Some of the more prominent ones include Ernie Els, Fred Couples, Bobby Jones, Byron Nelson, Gene Littler,

Bobby Nichols, Johnny Miller, Babe Zaharias, Carol Mann, Rory McIlroy, and, yes, John Daly. These professionals would've been good at any sport with their rhythmic, fluid, graceful swings. There was nothing contrived or manufactured in their swings. Each was a self-contained, homogenized blend of technique and art, particularly dance. They exhibited coordination as a cheetah does in the wild, chasing prey, as a shark does in the surf, hot on the heals of a pod of seals, as a red-tailed hawk does swooping down to pick up a brush rabbit.

There is something of ancient human beings in those swings, something free and unencumbered, something unburdened by the cog of decision, or the arrogance of developed muscle, or the hyperbole of a politician. The athletic swing sings an aria of near perfection. Its notes assemble into a symphony, so that from start to finish the observer sees it as one continuous piece, including even the silent spaces between the notes. Do athletic swings always work in relation to score on any particular round? As John Daly continually demonstrates, no. But they are a true expression of a golfer who swings that way out of something real in their nature. It is natural and organic, the athletic swing, not anything manufactured.

So what is it, exactly? What comprises the elements that are common to the athletic swing? For though it is so-called God given, there may be aspects of it that are already within the modern golfer but that have been battered down by instruction and technique. First, the athletic swing is one of motion. One of the key realms of the athlete, whether a curler or a downhill racer, is almost constant motion. Each sport has its prime examples. Willie Mays and Jackie Robinson in baseball. Michael Jordan and Bill Russell in basketball. Bo Jackson and Roger Staubach in football. Pele and Ronaldo in soccer. Jean-Claude Killy, Bode Miller, and Lindsey Vonn in skiing. And Roger Federer and Maria Sharapova in tennis.

In golf, you can spot an athletic swing right from the start. First is the waggle, a most neglected aspect of the modern swing. How many touring pros do you see waggle the golf club before swinging?

Practically none. What the waggle does is several things. But mostly it reduces tension that can build from anticipation of the swing and its results. In golf, we tend to be not so much task oriented as results oriented, and therein lies a basic problem. For any tension in the mind, i.e., anticipating a particular result, will lead to tension in the body. The so-called mind/body connection. Don't minimize it, folks. It's real. Any doubt, negativity, or thought of past failure will translate into a tightening of muscles throughout the body—muscles you weren't even aware you had. And, however subtle, any such tightening will intervene in the smooth rhythm, pace, and timing that a golf swing must have to be able to return a square club face to the ball at impact. To stand up to a ball at address, rock still, and start a swing without some preliminary motion is like a cat that doesn't move his tush before pouncing on a mouse. You just won't see that because cats know instinctually there has to be some waggle before the pounce.

So a waggle of some sort triggers the start of the swing. There is no exact formula as to how to waggle. You could copy a pro who does and try it out but I would suggest modifying it to suit your particular style and what feels right. I kind of shift my weight back and forth while moving my hands slightly into a forward press but I'd be hard pressed to describe it exactly as it happens. I'd recommend checking out Brandt Snedeker. Even his right thumb is involved in his athletic waggle and swing. It's a natural, tension-free movement, without thought, that sets my body in motion towards that key move that I've previously written about. It's a relatively slow movement that reminds the body that the backswing should be accomplished at the same pace as that waggle.

And that leads to the next key feature of the athletic swing: balance. For given the speed of the downswing and the length of the club, golf is a balance sport. Like the pendulum of a grandfather clock, the head remains steady while the body and arms swing around it. The downswing momentum of the club can easily pull you off balance, so the challenge is to maintain that balance as swing speeds vary between 70 and 120 miles per hour. If you've ever driven a car at those speeds, you know how fast that is; and if you jerk the wheel just a bit while driving that fast, you know how easy it is to lose control of that vehicle. The head is key, and if you watch films of Jackie Robinson stealing a base back in the day (or watch the movie *42*) you'll see that his head remained rock steady as he took his otherwise animated lead. Bode Miller, too, keeps that head relatively steady as he carves turns at unbelievable speeds on his downhill runs. So a slow backswing with a steady head, and an increasingly fast downswing with as steady a head as possible into impact is what to strive for (there will almost always be some head movement for a handicapper, and, as Tiger Woods shows on a vertical plane, for a top pro as well).

Finally, the athletic swing demonstrates full extension of the arms at impact after the weight has mostly transferred to the forward side. This swing is free-flowing and unencumbered of any tension, much like a child swinging a weighted rope, or a hammer thrower releasing her hammer at precisely the right moment throwing her entire body into the toss with a mighty yell with arms outstretched. Tennis players, too, achieve tremendous power from their core strength, with the arms stretched fairly straight at impact. Higher handicap golfers seem to panic at impact, decelerating by crooking the forward arm at impact, losing balance, poise, and power. It's poor etiquette to give a rebel yell at impact, but think of that hammer thrower, and extend your arms out toward the target as you come through the ball.

I've attempted to explain the athletic swing but I realize as I finish, that's it's more a feeling of grace, fluidity, and the power that results from those factors that lie at the heart of such a swing. For when you swing as such, and you make pure contact with the ball, you will experience such a feeling as you have never experienced before in any sport. It is the Holy Grail of golf—satisfying, complete, and rewarding in itself, regardless of result.

How to Make a Hole-in-One

OK, you got me. It's a headline known in the writing trade as a hook (not to be confused with the other use of the term in the golfing trade). But, as a golfer who has scored three of these gems—the last one being on Veterans Day, 2013, twelve days after I turned sixty-eight—I do have something concrete to contribute, thus transforming the title beyond the realm of shameless marketing.

First, realize that in golf, at its core, every shot is mutually exclusive of the ones before the present shot. In practice, that is often not the case. Memories stick to the present moment, hanging there like the underside of embroidery. That side is messy, complicated, while the finished side is smooth, unencumbered, and . . . well . . . finished. So when I approached the 5th hole at Adobe Creek in Petaluma, California, I was fresh off an ignominious double bogey on the short par-5 4th, my shoulders slumped, and self-deprecatory voices in my head. The underside of the embroidery was in full display as I grabbed a club for the 118-yard par 3, muttering profanities to myself every inch of the way to the tee box. At that moment, I took pause and reminded myself that I was hitting the ball pretty good that day. Solid contact. Good pace. Straight tee shots. On the previous hole, I'd hit the first two shots very well. The third was also solid but I'd picked the wrong wedge into a narrow green, which it flew. I then flubbed two chips and two putted for a double. But if I removed the chips, I'd played it well. Thinking this helped settle my judging mind, as I prepared to swing at the par-3 green. Becalmed, I hit the ball solidly, saw it bounce twice and disappear into the cup. And that's how to make a hole-in-one. What? Wait. That's it? There must be more, you're saying.

Well, no, essentially that is it. Anyone can make a hole-in-one in this game (no guarantees, of course) if you treat each shot mutually exclusive from anything before. Of course, you can still bitch and moan about a wayward shot, but the moment you step up and address the ball for the next shot, you must clear the mind of such verbal detritus, and be totally present with that next swing, executing the swing as if the delinquent shot never happened. That is the definition of total presence: that moment in time when the mind is focused on what it is doing without the burden of extraneous thought or judgment or even labeling of whatever it is you're doing. It is what Zen practice is all about. There's no dogma attached to it. There's no explanation needed for it. Tiger Woods has perhaps trivialized the expression, but it truly "is what it is."

Of course, you can increase your chances of making a hole-in-one if you swing the club properly, particularly if it's on plane. Now that concept baffles most amateurs, and even pros will drop and lose the "on plane" puzzle piece from time to time during their career. But if you can stay on plane during the entire swing, you are tantalizingly close to the Holy Grail of golf. It helps to get all the other fundamentals right as they put the body in the most advantageous and comfortable position to approach a swing that is, at its core, unnatural and awkward.

So, how to know if you are on plane? The best and simplest way comes from teaching pro Michael Breed. To make sure you're on plane in the early part of the swing, stick a tee in the little hole at the butt end of the grip, leaving about an inch and a half showing. Take the club back to where the wrists begin to cock, making sure the tee is pointing toward the target line and that you can see the tee. If so, you are on plane and are likely to stay on plane. If you can't see the tee, the shaft is too upright, and you are not on plane, with a poor prognosis for returning to the proper plane. As you complete the backswing, the arms stay connected to the chest, and the shoulders turn to maximum according to your individual ability. If the arms become disconnected from the chest or the left arm breaks down into a "chicken wing," you're likely to leave the proper plane, opening you up to trouble. This is when the club often goes beyond parallel at the top, something that should be avoided. As Englishman and touring pro Justin Rose advises, a shorter swing is better, building up a coiled tension, and making it easier to stay on plane. But the true beauty of Breed's tip is its simplicity, making it easy—you don't need the tee once you get used to where the butt of the club should be pointing—to check your position as part of your pre-shot routine. Canadian Mike Weir and Spaniard Beatriz Recari both utilize this technique before they pull the trigger.

What happens when you're on plane is that the ball will more likely go in the direction you are aiming. This is true since an on plane swing will likely result in a square clubface at impact. Whether you make solid contact depends too on weight shift, but that's something fairly easily corrected on the range. Starting and staying on plane greatly increases your chances of hitting the ball on a line to where you are aligned (please see the chapter "Align-iron-ment"). Whether it goes in the hole, depends on the club you picked, your wind calculations, the position of the pin, the relative humidity, earth's gravitational pull, luck, and . . . whether angels were available for golf ball hole-in-one duty for that particular day, time, and location.

Of course, you might also want to consider the curious case of Welshman Stuart Manley who moved into a share of second place in the second round at the 2013 World Cup with an ace on the 176-yard par-3 third using an 8-iron. He thought he'd won the snazzy car behind him but found out when he retrieved his ball that the car prize was only good on the last day of the tourney.

"I thought I had won the car, and the adrenalin was really pumping," Manley said. "The highest high to the lowest low. I heard some giggles . . . some laughs" from the crowd. Manley's approach on the next hole went into a greenside bunker, and his third shot went off the back of the green. When he chipped back on, his shot rolled off the front of the green and into a gully. From there, it took him four attempts to get the ball back on the green—it kept rolling back down to his feet—before he three-putted for an 11. He went then from second to a tie for fifteenth.

So you might want to wipe the slate clean of everything—good and bad shots—before approaching the next hole. Golf fortunes can change quickly . . . either way. And, as Manley discovered, hole-in-one angels can disappear in a flash.

Building and Maintaining Confidence

With golf, maintaining confidence throughout the round is a challenge. Regardless of what level of skill you're at, you will hit poor shots from time to time. Confidence rises and falls, ebbs and flows, and it all happens between the ears. You have to group and regroup continuously, not just for one type of shot, but for every club in the bag. For each club represents a different level of confidence. The other day at Rooster Run in Petaluma my driver was clicking on all cylinders: straight and, for me, long. I'd pull that club and knew exactly how I wanted to swing it. I knew where it was going to go. I knew I could rely on it: direction and distance. Ideally, that's what you want for every club in the bag. That day, I was confident with my driver. But a few holes later I had about ninety yards to the pin so I pulled my fifty-two-degree gap wedge. I have never felt comfortable with this particular club. It's a top brand, same as all my irons, but there is something in the weight of this gap wedge, which was purchased separately from the set, that was too heavy, almost clunky. Just a bit top heavy to remind me of the less than desirable results I've had with this club. The distance was right for this club since I'd tested it previously, but my brain equated the club with potential trouble. And sure enough, I screwed up the shot, knocking the ball left of the green leaving me a difficult chip. The chip went long and there was another dropped shot. There was just something about that club that affected my expectations and prognosis about where it would take me. A self-fulfilling prophecy, and very little confidence. Couldn't miss it with the driver. Couldn't make it with the gap wedge.

It was the first time I'd played Rooster in a number of years, and the greens were unexpectedly fast for a public course. I just couldn't figure out the speed for long putts over twenty-five feet, leading to too many three-putts, and little confidence. But the greens were running true and in great shape, so the shorter putts of fifteen feet and under, I handled well, and much more confident with them. Do you see what I'm getting at? You can have different levels of confidence depending on the specific condition, shot, or club required. Your goal is to maintain the confidence you already have and build confidence where you don't have it. So how to do that?

As for the confidence you have, just continue to play with that grooved swing for that particular club or shot on that particular day. I continued to use my key move on the backswing, which helped me keep the driver swing on plane and at the right pace throughout. Drive after drive went far and straight (with a couple exceptions).

IMPROVING

With chipping, my pitching wedge was working nicely: a bit too long at times because of the speed of the greens, but crisply struck. No stubs. Nothing thin. Confidence was high with my "chipping" wedge. However, I could not get my short irons going, often pulling them left and missing greens or putting myself in three-putt territory. Confidence was low with my scoring irons, and I dropped four to five strokes as a result. What this analysis required was to step back at some point and take inventory of how I was doing. To do that, I needed a fairly high degree of mindfulness to break out of the bubble created when we play golf. The bubble results in being too present, too focused, too concentrated when we are playing. Because when you're in the bubble, you can't see yourself and the mistakes you're making. You're mesmerized by what's around you: the birds, the breeze, the trees, the sound of birds—all the calming things that we don't normally pay much attention to in our runaround lives. In other words, you're feeling so good, so relaxed, that you forget to take inventory of your game that day, and cease making corrections.

Life is like that as well. When we are free of stress, and feeling no pain, on vacation for example, we don't look too closely at our lives. We don't take much of an inventory. But when life goes sour, we are then more motivated to examine why that is so and try to make amendments. An occasional sour shot in golf is often not enough an incentive to stop and analyze our game, looking for points of confidence or lack thereof. It's similar to slot machine psychology in a way: the machine makers make sure to give you an intermittent payout to keep you seated and playing more. All golfers have occasional good shots, which accomplish a similar payout. With mindfulness, however, nothing is too small to be noticed. Bad shot, good shot, flubbed shot, great shot. You record all of it by increasing your level of consciousness and awareness. That way, you begin to fine tune your game and level of confidence for various aspects of your game. In other words, if you're having a rough day, you'll need to step back, take inventory, and make adjustments more often than if you're having a good day.

Normally, we may have many swing thoughts to help us return to a favorable track. We only use one or two at a time, but if they are not working (because our bodies and minds may be affected by different conditions from day to day), then pause, take inventory, and try a different swing thought, even in mid-round. The other method is to avoid a club where you know your confidence is low, and use high confidence level clubs whenever possible. If I'm at 6-iron distance from the pin, and I have more confidence with my 7 then I do with my 6, the 7 might still get me on the green with a longer putt, whereas a botched 6 may not. Same thing with the drive. If you have more confidence with your 3-wood than your driver, your 3-wood may be a bit shorter and on the fairway, where the driver may be longer but in the trees. Go with the higher confidence club, and use the range to build confidence with the lower confidence clubs. You could also buy a new set, matched for weight and consistency.

You can build confidence through practice and experimentation. The brain/body connections get more comfortable and familiar the more you practice properly. Are you practicing properly? Part of this involves making an inventory of where you're losing strokes. And if you can't figure it out and are stuck in a mental morass, that's where a teaching pro can help. We go to a doctor for checkups from time to time. Go to a reliable teaching pro to make sure you're on track. Like an AA Member who leans on his or her sponsor, we golfers need to lean on our teaching pros on occasion on that road to recovery, confidence, and lower scores.

The Case for Less Practice and More Play

A few years ago I took on a demanding full-time job (after losing a higher-paying part-time job to Great Recession budget cuts), changing my life dramatically, including my golfing life. I no longer had the time or energy to practice as much as I had been. And a strange thing happened. I started hitting the ball more solidly and scoring better when I played, which was also much less than before. With practice, I tend to get very technical and mechanical, losing the natural feel and flow of my swing, ignoring that basic connection of my hands—those sensitive hands and fingers that virtually define us as human beings—on the grip. The hands send millions of signals to the brain that in turn sends commands to the body to act in specific ways. And at some point, we must give that communication free expression. Sure, there's a place for lessons and practice but if you get too mechanical, you risk losing that aspect of the game that relies on what we already know, but needs us to get out of our own way to see.

We practice to gain some sense of control over this impossible game. But sometimes we go too far and overload the body/mind/spirit with too much information, sometimes very confusing and conflicting information. We get frustrated at times, I know, and out of that frustration can come desperation. So we practice more. Or find a new instructor. Even Tiger Woods, despite his amazing record, wants to get better: so he changes swing coaches every few years, going into swing change mode, grinding his gears and juggling his swing thoughts, as he tries to right the ship after losing some imaginary edge. But somehow I think he'd be better off if he tried to figure it out himself. TMI. Too much information. Tiger's hands—just about the best hands in golf history—know how to get him back to the old Tiger. He needs to trust them.

Too much practice can also wreak havoc on the body. You get through one bucket and think you've got it. So you rush over and get another bucket. You rake those balls over like you go through a bag of potato chips. And the body starts getting sore and makes adjustments and adaptations, and that perfection that you seek gets lost in all the effort. That certain "it" that you seek. Then you go to the course for a round the next day and you try to regain that "it" that you came so close to and the mind and body and hands just can't quite remember what that "it" was. You spend the rest of the round noodling around for "it" but it's just not there. Parole denied: you've got to do more time at your present handicap.

So better to practice less and play more. It's easier on the body. It's more fun. And you may find your own hands are very good teachers.

HOLE 7
Adapting

F ROM ITS START, golf and golfers have adapted to the needs and customs of the day and location. Starting on links and dunes land by the sea, golf expanded into parklands, providing recreation for inland locations. At first, it was a walking game, subject to anything nature threw at it. Players adjusted and persevered and developed techniques and equipment to cope with mud, wind, rain, and ruts, no matter how extreme. Players moved along at a fast pace, considerate of those behind and in front. Today, even with motorized carts, play has slowed, sometimes agonizingly so. Numbers of golfers have diminished, discouraged by the time it takes to play, and the discourtesies of other less conscious players.

What Golf Needs and Doesn't Need

We hear a lot about what golf needs to thrive. First, let me say golf will survive now and for as long as people walk this beautiful earth. Golf will never not be. The bug was released the first time a Scotsman fashioned a club and struck a ball of some sort (see the late Robin Williams's very funny monologue on the origins of golf on YouTube). Others saw this, tried it for themselves, heard and felt a certain *clickit,* or *thrump*, or *wommpit* (no matter how hard I try, I don't think I could ever find the right word to describe a well-hit golf shot), and needed to try that again. Golf is not a sport or game: it's a habit, and it embeds deep within. My father tried to play golf but his huge ego wouldn't allow it. It's a humbling game and those with overly prominent egos don't humble well. Golf will pulverize an ultra-ego. My dad gave his Bobby Jones signature clubs to me and inadvertently got me started on a lifelong journey. I was the first in my family to play the game and would have turned pro if I'd gotten any support to do so. But once I'd experienced the exhilaration of a finely hit golf shot, I was hooked, and have stayed hooked (with a short time on the wagon) for almost sixty years.

So not to worry about the fate of the game. As long as a ball stings the sweet spot of a club from time to time, the game will remain intact. It might ebb and flow according to the vicissitudes of society, TV ratings may vary according to whether Rory is in the field, golf courses may go bankrupt, but golf will endure. There are, though, a few things that golf needs and doesn't need.

1. Power carts. Seeing a couple of twenty-five-year-old yahoos in carts is an abomination of what golf was intended to be. Golf was and is a game on foot. Golf and walking are synonymous. Golf was meant to slow you down, take a break from the workaday world, relax, enjoy nature, consider your next shot, talk with your boon companions, and yes, keep up the pace so as not to impede those behind you, but not to dart about like rabbits running from predators. Then, often the starter puts those in carts and those walking in the same foursome. Again, a bad idea. Some go slow. Some go fast. Neither are satisfied. Make courses walkable. In fact, favor walkers, like at Bandon Dunes Golf Resort in southern Oregon; that is, have greens as close as possible to subsequent tees, just like the old courses in Scotland. Of course, I'm prejudiced around the pleasures and benefits of walking: after all, I wrote *The Mindful Hiker*!

2. Allowing rank beginners on the course with experienced players. When people who don't know the game are put on the course, a

great opportunity is lost. I know courses need to make money, but why not have an orientation where some of the fundamentals of etiquette and rules could be taught? This would at least speed play, reduce rude behavior and ignorance, and increase safety, setting a good foundation for a positive experience. Before renting a kayak on open waters, an orientation and safety class is often required. Such a requirement would also stress the importance of lessons, increasing business for the local pro.

3. Practice facilities. It's a game that needs lots of practice for all kinds of shots. We need grass tees, bunkers, chipping areas, putting greens, pitching areas. We need par-3 practice courses. The best that I've seen is at Bandon Dunes Golf Resort with its state of the art practice area. The worst is at most municipal courses. The solution is to tell your local pro what you need. Chipping and pitching areas are the parts of the game most lacking in facilities; and when they're there, they're too small, allowing only one or two golfers at a time. The reason, of course, is that courses make no money from chipping and pitching, since you don't need to buy a bucket to use them. Golf courses are commercial propositions, but best marketing practices should make it obvious that drawing people in to practice will make better golfers, who play that particular course more regularly. Let's change penny-wise, pound-foolish policies around practice facilities.

4. Drainage. Again, it takes money to make money. If courses don't drain well, golfers will not play there. Conditions are too sloppy; balls plug and are lost easily. It's hard enough to play this game in ideal conditions. Add proper drainage systems.

5. Unreasonably long par 4s on public courses. Have more short, yet challenging, par 4s. The pros are doing this with their driveable par 4s, and these holes are no cinch. Fans love them since they are risk-reward. Amateurs love them since they offer good opportunities to make par or better (of course, with water or sand in play, big numbers are possible too, but at least on the tee you think you have a chance at glory).

6. Unreasonable rules. For USGA and PGA events keep the rules as they are. For the rest of us, make it an option: play winter rules

anywhere, anytime. Preferred lies on the fairway will speed up play. Scores and handicaps will go down. It's a different game for the low, mid, and high handicappers. This will level the playing field, still producing legitimate handicaps. We have to make this game easier if we want to attract and keep people playing. Playing it as it lies is fine for pros, amateur competitions, and the ghost of Wee Bobby Jones, but it sets the bar too high for casual, recreational play. Other rules could be modified as well to acknowledge the difference between competitive and recreational play. It's called bifurcation of the rules, and it could help save golf from attrition.

7. The standard of an eighteen-hole round. Courses need to offer more options to people with less time, less money, and less physical ability to play eighteen holes. Golf needs three-hole, nine-hole, and twelve-hole options, with corresponding fee rates. It needs lunchtime options. It needs state of the art practice area options, where instead of playing the course, you can opt to pay a fee (in addition to a bucket of balls) to practice for a certain period of time. Let's get with it, club professionals. Get creative! You can do more than sell balls, clubs, and shirts.

8. How about a new game of Two Ball or Mulligan Golf, where you get the option of playing a second ball over either nine or eighteen holes of play. If you hit your first into the woods, fugetaboutit, as they might say in New York. Keep the play moving by playing another instead. Of course, if your first shot is to your liking, play it. Many amateurs already do this, though, guiltily. It's called the Mulligan. Of course, this would only apply to recreational golf and would not qualify for posting a score for a handicap. But so what? Most golfers don't need or want a handicap. My friend Rob suggested an interesting variation to this new game: a reverse Mulligan where you can call for an opponent to play a good shot over again. It's a bit like bringing back the stymie where you could purposefully block your opponent's putt with your ball.

These suggestions are, by no means, conclusive, but merely a starting point for discussion. Golf needs adjustments to keep it alive, thriving, more playable, and more fun. It needs to attract more kids, more women, more baby boomers, and more elders. We golfers need to discuss the issues that affect our hallowed avocation and, for some, vocation. Golf needs reforming to meet the demands and trials of this new century.

Thoughts on the Rules of Golf

Americans don't like rules much. Generally, we follow them but we gripe along the way. They're usually written in fine print or in legalese or in laws that we didn't even know existed, so we don't bother following them to the letter. We look for ways around them, hoping that our infractions are so miniscule that no one will notice. In sports, there are penalties for breaking rules. In football you can lose yards or have touchdowns can-celed; in basketball there are foul shots; in baseball you can get thrown out of the game; in soccer there are penalty kicks; in horse-racing you can get disqualified; and in golf there are penalty strokes.

In golf, I've seen amateurs, including myself, break the rules in friendly games, like giving oneself a preferred lie on occasion, but gen-erally follow them in competition. For a touring pro, the rules of golf are sacrosanct and knowing them is part of his or her profession. Like a lawyer who must know the rules of the courtroom to be effective, the golf pro must know the universal rules of golf as well as any local rules that apply to that particular course. It's his or her responsibility to know and understand the rules before play begins. Not doing so opens the player to tremendous risk, as Dustin Johnson found out a couple years ago at the PGA Championship, one the year's four majors. Pundits, players, and fans will be talking about that one for years, but it offers a good lesson for those who seriously take on this demanding game. If you break the rules, knowingly or unknowingly, you take a penalty—often a self-imposed penalty. For an amateur, the risk is slight: nothing but one's pride is on the line. But for a pro, who makes a living playing in tournaments, the risks are huge, with championships and big money on the line.

Dustin Johnson's ball was sitting on sand for his second shot on the 18th hole at Whistling Straits. That sand was clearly defined as a designated bunker and not a haphazard waste area where one could ground a club. If he had looked around and seen the posted notices in the locker room, he, or his caddie, would've known that. The penalty was justified when he grounded his club.

Once again, the mind reared its head to affect a golf tournament and a player. If Johnson had been more aware, more mindful, he would have known about this rule dictating the course's 1,200 bunkers. Part of the profession of being a golf caddie is knowing the rules thoroughly, and not just being a statistician having all the yardages in a little book in his back pocket. Golf is a peculiar game in that respect, in that rules can be added by the local venue. Tennis can't do that, nor can soccer, or lacrosse, or water polo. So the pro must take the time to study all the nuances that golf presents. Or, if he doesn't, he needs to ask for rulings by the officials out on the course during a tournament. Dustin Johnson didn't ask and he lost an opportunity to win a major.

Golf offers great lessons for living one's life. And one of them is to consider deeply—in business, in marriage, in work, in relationships, in finances, on the road—the rules of engagement and the consequences for breaking them. Rules are not made to be broken: they are made to be understood and followed, or challenged in an appropriate and mature way if you disagree with them. Golf is one of the only examples in our society where the standard is to call a penalty on yourself when you knowingly break a rule. That is a noble and civilized standard. The bar really doesn't get much higher. So golf contributes to building an entirely moral society, one that ultimately needs no enforcers of the rules. The golf pro is the guardian of that standard, and holds his head high after seeing and calling an infraction on himself, even though, as a result, he loses the game.

On Bifurcation: New Suggested Rules for the Recreational Golfer

So what is golf for you: a competitive sport or a recreational game? Golf as sport is competitive, such as the professional tours, such as your weekend money match, such as your club championship. Ken Venturi's father wanted his son to see golf as competitive and told him when he started out: play quickly, and count every stroke. Play it as it lies. Play to win. Follow all the rules, even calling penalties on yourself. Young Ken shot 172 his first time out at Harding Park in San Francisco. I'm sure Earl Woods told Tiger something similar, as did Deacon Palmer instruct Arnold, and Jack Grout told Jack Nicklaus. When you approach golf as a competitor, you play it as it was played in Old Tom Morris's day, in Harry Vardon's day, in Bobby Jones's day, and Byron Nelson's day. You play it according to the same rules that all competitors play it by. You keep score. Every stroke.

I know previously I've extolled the virtues of playing the ball as it lies, but when golf as a game is something fun you do on a Saturday afternoon with like-minded companions, whether friends or total strangers, if your ball lands in a divot, you bump it out without penalty. You play winter rules all year round, whether it is in Palm Springs or Boston. Winter rules mean you can lift, clean, and place your ball; you can prop up your ball in the fairway to give yourself a preferred lie. It's not traditional golf, but it's more realistic for unskilled players who will never compete or even hold a handicap. It's a way to keep them playing the game, and playing faster than they presently do.

Now I know some of you will take exception with what I'm writing here, but golf needs an infusion of new ideas and energy. Too many are dropping out or not even attempting to play. And when they do play, they play too slowly and without consciousness of those around them, much to the consternation of more skilled players who then think of dropping the game themselves. Courses do little to help the situation, only interested in those who come through the door with money in their hand. The current rules and specs have mostly been designed for professionals and advanced amateurs: they don't translate well to the weekend hacker who slows the game for all the other recreational players. Let's take playing the ball as it lies, for example. The pros play on layouts manicured to perfection, far better than the public courses most of us play. These public courses are maintained poorly as a rule. Faced with poor lies, even in the fairway, unskilled amateurs have little hope of making a decent shot. This is not fun. Not fun, at all. And without golf being fun, what's the point of playing? What motivated the founders of the game? Competition, yes. Betting, sure.

But fun must have been at the core of their desire to do something with their free time. Certainly that was true of the Scottish nobles who were bored silly with all their money but nowhere to go and not much, save drink, to spend it on. Having fun was the main motive. Today, especially among us non-nobles, there are often better, more enjoyable, ways of spending five hours on any given day. So the average golfer, and even some pros who are getting older, give it up, and go fishing, or whatever they consider more fun, or relaxing, or productive, or ego-enhancing, or meditative.

So what I suggest is at the first tee players decide whether they are playing by the official rules of golf or each player chooses whatever rules he or she is playing by, and their score is private and irrelevant to any other player in the foursome. If a player considers it a practice round, they may give themselves preferred lies in fairways or may practice playing it as it lies, especially if planning to enter a competition or they are keeping an official handicap, which would require playing by the official rules. As the pros do during practice rounds, they may play an extra shot or two if it doesn't hold up play, perhaps with an old ball that doesn't require taking time to find if mis-hit. People do this anyway now, so why not make it OK. There's no loss of integrity or ethics since such a round is not competitive in any way. If the foursome, or even just two people in the group, decides the round is competitive, and that could be just for a beer at the end, they can declare what rules they will play by: preferred lies or play it as it lies, or winter rules, or pars only counted, or match play, or whatever. Since it is not an officially sanctioned event, the players can modify the rules.

Of course in official competitions players would follow the rules set up by those sponsoring the tourney, and this includes local rules peculiar to that particular course, such as the aforementioned Whistling Straits at the PGA Championship in 2010 where Dustin Johnson apparently did read the local rules in the locker room. Official handicaps would remain vital to such competitions. And they could be important to golfers who just want to measure their progress as they work toward improvement. So courses needn't worry about losing too much business under these proposed changes. Even the Old Course at St. Andrews, golf's original home, requires that players carry and use small artificial mats to hit shots from the fairway to protect the fragile turf during winter months. Can a traditionalist post a handicap using such local rules on the most famous course in the world? I don't know for sure, but I doubt it. What would Bobby Jones have said?

What these new rules do is legitimize and bring into the open what many golfers do already, on the sly. So when it comes time to compare scores at the 19th hole, a companion can openly point out to his friend who has scored lower, "Of course, *I* was playing by the official rules and *you* weren't." That places on the table what is usually a source of hidden contempt and irritation that is the current situation in informal competition.

So it brings choice into play among golfers who are playing the game for varying reasons. The weekend hacker no longer has to struggle with rules that are designed for an accomplished player. I do not believe this undermines the spirit of the game. On the contrary, flexible rules will bring more people into the game, further enriching the ball and club manufacturers, increasing demand for more and better designed golf courses (the six courses at Bandon Resorts including the new putting course called the "Punchbowl" are fine examples of making golf more fun while maintaining high standards), and making the game more appealing and faster to play.

Golf has evolved since it started and needs to continue to evolve to match the mores and needs of the current culture. These suggested rules allow individual recreational golfers to make a choice. The criteria are simple: Are you playing competitively or recreationally? With the former, you follow the established rules of golf. With the latter, you decide what rules you'll follow.

HOLE 8
Life Lessons

GOLF AND LIFE often run parallel and intersect. In the course of eighteen holes, much is required of the golfer, mentally and physically. There are unpredictable challenges, which call for an adaptable mind and a body able to repeat a reliable, predictable swing. Any lapse in concentration can translate in poor results, and how one deals with poor results on the course, as in life, is often the measure of character and the attainment of success.

Guts, Glory, and Plasticity of Mind

How many times have you scored a triple bogey and essentially given up on the round? I've even stopped keeping score I've been so demoralized. Keegan Bradley, after chipping into the water, had a triple on the 15th hole on the last day of the 2011 PGA Championship—the first major he'd ever played in—and came back to win the tournament. That takes guts and courage and the ability to never say die, traits any golfer could use more of. These are traits of the mind, traits of character, traits of a person who can turn adversity into the seed of an equal or greater benefit. After Bradley's triple, he was five shots behind Jason Dufner, who was, at the time, a thirty-four-year-old journeyman golfer. Bradley then birdied his next two, one with a forty-foot putt, and parred the 18th, arguably the most difficult hole on tour. He tied Dufner in regulation, a gutsy feat that has to be one of the great comebacks in the history of the majors. How he did it is a lesson we can all learn from.

Simply said, in golf, as in life, you never give up. Golf tests the resiliency of the mind, the brain, to come back after disaster. The brain is conditioned generally to give up rather than come back and try again. It's an organ of memory and we tend to remember the bad more than the good. Think PTSD, which is near epidemic in this country. So instead of facing obstacles and hindrances, we often give up and go in another direction. Or we medicate ourselves with whatever opiate is at hand. The brain's amygdala, the center of emotional response, is often so conditioned by the time we reach adulthood that it forgets its original function: to help us get through tough times, times of change, times of negativity, of disappointment, of disruption to our comfort zone. The amygdala becomes dysfunctional, and requires external booster shots to help us through the day.

When disaster hits in golf, and it will whether you are Rory McIlroy or John Doe, how you respond is critical. In 1990, unknown Mike Donald was on the verge of winning the U.S. Open. He lost in a playoff against Hale Irwin and was never heard from again until he emerged on the Champions Tour in 2005. Ben Hogan, on the other hand, almost died in a head-on car crash in 1949, then came back and won six more majors. And I shot 45 going out at Bennett Valley the other day, and then came in with a 37. In golf, you never say die. You can catch fire at any point but you must be in control of your mind to do so. So how can you accomplish this in a culture that assaults the mind until it is ground into submission, that conditions the mind to kowtow to the flavor of the day?

First, you have to find your center. The Japanese consider the belly, the hara, to be the center of one's being. They developed a meditation that focuses the breath on the hara. As the breath comes in, the belly expands: As the breath goes out, the belly contracts. This is the polar opposite of the way most Westerners breathe. Try it. You'll see what I'm talking about. When disaster hits in golf, like a skulled chip shot for example, the breath gets short. Anger and frustration arise. You throw the club to the ground. You curse. You look to the sky. Touring pros pull their cap down over their eyes a lot. You've blown a shot, and the enslaved amygdala is in irons. You go to the next tee and you're still fuming.

Keegan Bradley went to the next tee after chipping into the water for a triple, and he proceeded to birdie the hole. He regrouped. He focused on making a good swing. This is an emotional guy, unlike some of the automatons on tour. He breathed, reining himself in. This is important. He reined himself in. The mind tends to take off in situations like this like the runaway stagecoach in old TV Westerns. And how did the hero stop the stagecoach? He bravely jumped on the horses and pulled in the reins. In golf, you need to jump on your neurons and gain control of your thinking, which includes your emotions. You need to treat every hole as if it were the first hole, without memory or influence of any hole before it.

This is called plasticity of mind—the ability of the mind to break through the calcification of conditioning and bend like a willow to whatever condition that arises. It's how human beings have survived and thrived through all these years of evolution. And it's how golfers survive double and triple bogeys. Plasticity of mind is critical for the golfer. Conditions change rapidly during the course of a round of golf. Expectations turn sour. Our best efforts go south. Every shot has the potential to go awry. Bouncing back is integral to good scoring. And good scoring is golf's Grail. So how does one achieve this plasticity of mind?

There is only one way: to dive into the maelstrom and take golf head on; to get battered around and beaten down; to feel the fire and not back down. The atrophied amygdala must be thrown into that fire in order to melt the ice around its edges. The conditioning has to be broken and the only way to do that is to go into the fray, into the source of nervousness and trepidation. It will not always be smooth.

It will not always work. But the amygdala will eventually get used to acting on its own, with heightened confidence in its ability to face hardship. Like a battle-toughened soldier, it will not hesitate to take on the enemy. And in golf, the enemy is clear: it is none other than one's own mind and its tendency to lapse into negativity and despair.

Meditation is a useful tool in gaining plasticity of mind. But it is not the be-all, end-all solution. Buddhists call meditation "the Practice," but at some point you have to leap into the abyss of life, with full faith that you will survive, and that your own mind will support you in the journey. Golf is good practice for living one's life as a fully conscious human being, for it takes both guts and plasticity of mind to come back from a triple bogey and win a major . . . or an opening 45 with a 37 coming home.

What Golfers can Learn from Skier Bode Miller

Several years ago, alpine skier Bode Miller was a goat in the public eye. He came up winless in the 2006 Winter Olympics after high expectations. More recently, Miller has won a number of medals and is a hero again. The catch is, Bode doesn't give a damn either way. He skis 100 percent, regardless of results, not competing for medals or accolades, but for the fun of the sport. He skis in, and for, the moment, with abandon, and caring not what people think of him. He is a true Zen athlete, a pure athlete, who despite many injuries and falls, gets up and tries again, sometimes winning, sometimes losing. I commend Bode Miller for having the courage for being his own man in the face of stinging public opinion. He is not a role model for kids, nor does he try to live up to others expectations, nor does he hold back in competition. He's been called crazy, reckless, selfish, irresponsible, and immature. And, yes, in all probability, he has been all of those. Yet, Bode Miller is his own man, living his own life. Maybe fatherhood has changed him, or marriage, or renewed dedication to his teammates and country. He eschews the American values of the "winning a medal or you're nothing" approach, enhancing his public image, acting like a man, and such nonsense. He has courage, both as an athlete, and as a human being. After one of his winning runs, he said, "I came out of the gate ready to risk it all. It feels great to have that freedom. I'm free to ski right now. The way I ski is without regard for consequence. If you can do that in these big Games, you get rewarded."

In golf, we've seen similar examples of professionals who get up and try again. The penultimate golfer was Bobby Jones, who overcame anger issues early in his career, highlighted by walking off the course after a series of bad shots in an English tournament, to winning the Grand Slam then retiring from competitive golf forever at twenty-eight years of age. The public was shocked, wanting more of Jones, but after years of stress and pressure-related illnesses, he'd had enough, despite unequaled success. He too was his own man, living life on his own terms. In later life, despite a crippling disease, he showed great integrity and an enduring honoring of the game.

In the modern era, David Duval is another example of one who keeps courageously trying in the face of failure. Steve Stricker fell from a faulty driver swing, to almost quitting the game, to coming back and becoming number two in the world at one point. Champions Tour pro Bernhard Langer has defied age, often showing true grit, playing high-level golf and continuing to win as a senior. Englishman Ian Poulter has displayed this kind of spirit in winning a WGC championship in the United States, and helping Europe win the Ryder Cup in the face of certain defeat. Poulter plays golf for golf's sake, happy to be swinging a club. He plays like Bode Miller skis. On the other hand, there was Sergio Garcia several years ago spitting into a cup after missing a putt, showing little respect for the players behind him and the game as a whole.

For amateurs, I would give the same advice, myself included: play golf for golf's sake. Mindless golf. No worries about score. play for fun. No concern about what your friends say. Play your own game, and play with as much skill and integrity as possible. Have at most one swing thought, and if that doesn't work, don't think at all. If you hit a lousy shot, go find it, and hit it again, thanking the golf gods for granting you the physical capacity to play this great game. Think of

Bode Miller, whether it was no medals in Turin or gold in Vancouver. Be a golfer, and do the best you can in any given moment.

The Intimidation Factor

The great intimidators in golf history are legendary: Walter Hagen, Bobby Jones, Ben Hogan, Byron Nelson, Sam Snead, Babe Zaharias, Arnold Palmer, Patty Berg, Jack Nicklaus, Mickey Wright, Nick Faldo, Greg Norman, Annika Sorenstam, Bernhard Langer, Hale Irwin, Tiger Woods, and . . . Eddie, the guy from Ireland I played with recently. That's right: we deal with intimidation even among amateurs on the muni all the time. There's the guy who plays the black or blue tees while we tiptoe up to the whites. Then there's the gorilla who cracks it 280 down the middle . . . just about every time. And the guy who keeps making par after bloody par while we scratch out bogeys. We're impressed. We're embarrassed. We're humiliated. We're intimidated. "I'm very intimidated," comedian Ray Romano said to swing coach Hank Haney, "by anyone who is very good at anything."

So we start to press, get fast at the top, lose our rhythm, and ultimately forget the swing we brought from the range earlier that day. We are playing the other guy's game, and the worse we score the more discouraged and demoralized we get. Eddie was a good guy and playing companion, but he started getting to me with his long accurate drives, his incessant pars, and the fact that he took up the game just a few years ago. That always gets me: the single-digit handicap golfer who "took up the game only a few years ago" while I've been playing since I was fourteen and often struggling. He keeps stats like an accountant too: fairways hit, greens in reg, putts per round. I sometimes don't even bother to put my score down.

So how to handle the intimidation factor? Well, Bobby Jones just kept hammering away at "Old Man Par," and defeated Hagen any number of times. Club pro Jack Fleck denied Ben Hogan his fifth U.S. Open in 1955 by bearing down and playing his own game. Jack Nicklaus was the only one who knew Arnold could be beaten, and the Golden Bear dominated The King for years. Patty Berg didn't let a dominant personality and tremendous talent stop her from defeating The Babe numerous times over the years of their competition. Twenty-year-old amateur Francis Ouimet, with the help of his ten-year-old caddie, Eddie Lowry, defeated Harry Vardon and Ted Ray, two of England's greatest and master intimidators in 1913 to win the U.S. Open. In other words, these players played within themselves, never letting the dominant player drag them out of their own rhythm and pace. They continually reminded themselves that they were playing against the golf course and not any particular player.

Golf is a unique game of mind, body, and spirit, and each element must be acknowledged and honed. It is a game of psychology. Eddie wore me down mentally when we played at Bennett Valley. What I should have done was go inward, focus, cut my swing speed down to 80 percent, and forget about Eddie when I was addressing the ball.

That's when golf, as we know it, ends, and something meditative, something mindful, something almost mystical, begins. That's when intimidation can't touch us.

Cultivating Patience

You've heard it said time after time by touring pros: I just have to be patient, when asked what their plan is for the upcoming round. But what exactly does that mean, especially in a society where few people seem to know what it means to be patient? How many patient drivers have you seen lately? How many patient fans have you seen at the ballpark? Who's patient at the DMV? And what about the foursome behind you? Were they patient when you last checked?

It is no easy thing to be patient. It has long been a virtue, as Emerson wrote in the mid-nineteenth century, "Adopt the pace of nature; her secret is patience." I learned about patience on Buddhist retreats, during long periods of sitting meditation where all you do is watch your own breath. You sit there for hours at a time observing the in-breath, then the out-breath. Nowhere to go. Nothing to do. Being patient takes on a whole new level of meaning. You want to move, go somewhere, and do something, as we've been trained to do in life, but you don't. You "stay patient" as most of the pros say in the post-round interviews.

For the amateur, patience is perhaps even more crucial. The pro knows he's capable of making birdie on every hole, so after a blow up-big number hole, he figures he can get it back at some point during the round, if he can maintain his cool. The middle or high handicap amateur is more apt to lapse into despair after a triple bogey or higher, knowing that the round is lost, doomed. You can spot him with head lowered, shoulders rounded, his pace that of a defeated homeless beggar. The bad hole is followed by more errant shots, as patience becomes no more than a vague theory, lying on the ground like heavy fog. So how does the average golfer cultivate patience?

What's critical is to know that golf is a thinking person's sport. True, when you pull the trigger for your swing, it's best to have a relatively clear (and steady) head; but before the swing happens, you have an opportunity to think through the shot. And that takes some modicum of patience when looking at all the options. The prime patience-building consideration involves something most of us only know from experience with gambling casinos, and a very poor training ground they are. It is the whole area of risk-reward. In the casinos, we take the risk and, more often than not, we lose our shirts. In golf, we often "go for it" and also not only lose our shirts but our golf balls as well. When faced with a tough shot, it takes patience to assess the possible risks and rewards in a very brief period of time. I could glibly say that it's best to always opt for less risk, but all of you know it's not that easy. Golfers are optimists by nature. We see a challenging shot and imagine we are Arnold or Phil or Seve or Tiger pulling it off and getting the congratulations of our playing companions. We imagine achieving the glory of clearing the lake or bunker and sticking it next to the pin. And when we pull it off, that's when amateurs feel what the pros feel (golf being one of the only sports where that's possible).

So yes, sometimes it's right to take chances, but only after you've made a careful assessment of the consequences if the shot goes badly. If the shot doesn't go as well as hoped for, the patient golfer will accept the outcome, find his ball, take the penalty, and assess the next shot with the same patience as the previous one. In that way, you learn about being patient from trial and error, one shot, one round, one season at a time. You learn how to let go of a bad shot, instead of beating yourself up for the rest of the round. Like Emerson's nature after a storm, you take the hit, feel it, express that feeling, then let it go and move on, and, after a time, the forest is healthier than before.

That's patience, and that's why the pros put such a high value on it. Any continuation of negative thoughts, and they miss the cut or lose a three-shot lead on Sunday afternoon, or let a whole season, or career, go into the tank. We've seen this most graphically with pros like David Duval, Anthony Kim, Michael Campbell, and Yani Tseng, all of whom have been at the top of their game, and then tumbled.

Of course, one of my tenets is that golf mimics life, so if you can attain patience on the golf course, it will extend to everyday events like freeway driving, dealing with your kids, coping with an overbearing boss, communicating with your spouse, standing in a long grocery store line, and forgiving ourselves for the unskillful things we do at times. Patience can be practiced and honed daily in whatever you do, as long as you remember to do so.

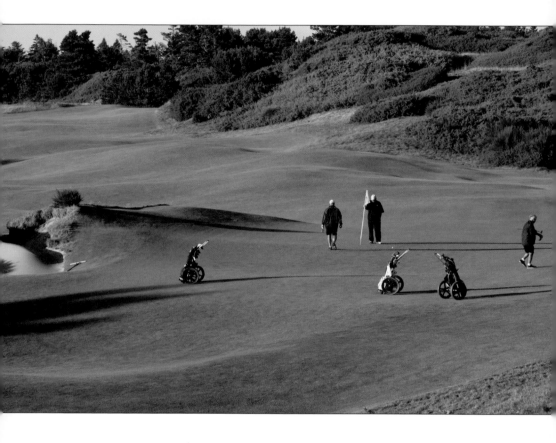

HOLE 9

The Dance Floor

PUTTING IS, PERHAPS, the most meditative aspect of golf, and can reveal more about the inner workings of a golfer than anything else connected with the game. Golfers refer to severe putting woes as "the yips," and there is an actual twitching involved, born of anxiety and tension and ambition denied.

Rolling the Rock when the Rock won't Roll

A few years ago, Aussie Jason Day hit a totally fat tee shot in Hawaii that went about fifty yards, then screwed up his approach, then reached the green about twenty-five feet from the cup, and then proceeded to drop the putt for a par. A good putt can salvage a lousy hole like a grand slam homer when your team's down 3-0 in the bottom of the ninth. Three flubs and a bomb can get the golf gods dancing around your head, breathing new life into a ho-hum round. That's the point of never letting golf get you down: a great putt may be just over the horizon.

And despite the golf pundits, putting doesn't require a huge amount of technique. You take the shortest, most easily controllable club in the bag, line it up square to the intended line of roll, judge how hard to hit it, and strike it right in the sweet spot center of the putter face.

If it doesn't fall in the cup, do the same thing and hit it again. One of the most important things is to find the right line, which depends on the contours of green between you and the hole. It's true that the head and most of the rest of the body need to be still during the motion, but you don't have to get too compulsive about it.

Putting is more feel than anything else. If you look at the great putters in history—Jones, Locke, Palmer, Player, Casper, Crenshaw, Nicklaus, Seve, Woods—they had different styles, different mechanics, and different dispositions. The one common element was confidence. When that left them, they hung up their clubs or were on the way out. Confidence is a mental characteristic developed by physical performance. Whether it be making love or playing golf, confidence builds or drops according to how well you play. Since putting is a separate game within golf, how well you play it depends on the numbers: one-, two-, or three-putt greens. When you know you can drop putts consistently from three to five feet, you can roll it boldly with your long lag putt. No problem. You know the line. You know the weight of your putter head and how far back to bring it. You know its sweet spot. And you know the kind of stroke that's best for you. That's confidence.

Of course, the exasperating thing about putting is that you can lose confidence. We saw that with Tiger Woods in 2010. Arguably, the greatest putter who ever lived lost his touch from three to ten feet. The greatest reader of greens of all time was not properly reading his short putts. His mind was somewhere else. His spirit was deflated. His confidence was depleted. Breaks and pace. Pace and breaks. The two have to mesh to get a putt to drop. And if you don't believe in your ability to piece these parts together, if the results of your efforts are not bearing fruit, if you're out buying yet another putter to solve the problem, you could have a serious case of, if not the yips, than a lapse in confidence.

To regain confidence with the putter, you have to experiment with your own equipment and your relationship with that equipment. Do you like your putter? Is it like an old friend or more like your dentist? Does it feel like a sledgehammer or a mop handle or a perfectly balanced wand? Do you labor behind the putt for interminable minutes trying to decide which way it will break? My suggestion would be to wipe the slate clean, the slate being your brain. On a practice green without too many breaks, grab the putter you normally use, give yourself about fifteen seconds tops to read the putt, take your address with your eyes directly over the ball, and give it a rap. Do that about twenty to thirty times, from about fifteen feet, seeing if you're getting close to the line and the pace, particularly the pace. When the pace improves, work on the line, trying different putts from different spots and distances on the practice green. Don't worry about dropping putts at this point. That will come. Just get them close and start to feel your ability to do so increase. You just want to avoid three-putts at this point. Three-putts are the absolute major cause of a loss of confidence around putting for an amateur. Shock a rat when he presses a bar to get food, and after a time you have a very screwed up rat.

After a while—I can't say how long—your confidence will return, as quietly and quickly as it left. Get out of your own way and let it return. As an old Buddhist teacher of mine always said, "All things arise and pass away." And, as with confidence with the putter, though it takes an element of faith, they arise again.

Reading Greens

As controversy swirls around the anchored putter, one fact remains: no matter how good or reliable your stroke is, you have to read the putt correctly. And reading the putt involves both speed and direction. Reading speed and direction involves feel. And feel involves confidence. All of these must be working perfectly for the putt to have much of a chance to go in. That, by the way, lest we forget, is the ultimate goal of any putt. Of all the above factors confidence is the most important, and it should only be governed by the golfer's mind, not by the technique of a putter anchored against the body, especially on the competitive level. The whole purpose of lining up a putt and figuring out its speed and direction is to give you confidence that determines how hard you hit the putt. For it's the force of your blow that determines how far the ball goes beyond the hole. Even if your direction is off a bit, if your speed is right, you won't have much of a putt coming back.

The greatest green reader of all time, with the possible exception of Young Tommy Morris, was Tiger Woods from 2000 to 2008. That and his distance control with short irons accounted for most of his fourteen major wins. I don't think Woods ever saw a putt, during that period, he didn't think he could make. He was in a state of mind beyond mortal confidence. Nothing could touch the state of mind he was in. He got to the point where his performance even decreased the confidence of other competitors. They figured his ten-footer would drop even before it dropped. And it usually did drop! That kind of success gets into your competitors' heads, and any stray thought that enters the head of a player who is putting is bound to lead to doubt, which leads to indecision, which translates to the nerve endings of the hands and fingers and thumbs. You'll sink a few, but not nearly enough to win.

Clearing the mind is what the Buddha did on an early December morning about 2,500 years ago. Once he got his pace and direction down, nothing could stop him as he sat beneath a fig tree, finally opening his eyes and the seeing the face of freedom in the morning star at dawn. He woke up, which is what the word Buddha means, and no problem would affect him as before. If Buddha had been a golfer, living in a later time, he would have won everything in sight.

So how do you attain this state of equanimity where you sink more putts than you miss? Let's back up a bit, for in golf, how you hit the previous shot often affects how you will hit your present shot. So first, hit your approach shot as close to the hole as you possibly can. A subsequent putt is better than a chip. And a twenty-foot putt is better than a fifty-foot putt. A three-foot putt after a chip is better—much better—than a fifteen-footer for par. So one key way to increase your putting confidence is to improve your approach game, your chipping game, and your lag putting game. Most pros are good with their short irons, around the greens, and at putts from five feet and in, so they can power a twenty-five-footer a few feet past, making sure they reach the cup, and have confidence they will sink the comeback putt, especially if they've watched the line as the ball passes the hole. Since there usually isn't much break right around the hole, they can then hit short putts firmly, (unless it's severely downhill) putting through any minor break.

Second, concentrate on feeling your putting speed. Some say good putters are born not made, and I think this is true. But you can practice getting a feel for distance. My suggestion would be to experiment with a backswing about as long as the forward stroke. Hit it on the center of the putter face, feeling and hearing a distinctive solid hit and sound. Your objective is to hit the ball hard enough to get it past the hole by about eighteen inches. That's a virtual tap-in and doesn't cause your knees to knock. Now, at first, this may result in more three-putts than you bargained for, but patience will be rewarded in time. For each time you go too far past the hole, that feel is registering in your nerve endings. Experiment on the practice green. Purposefully, hit it too hard on purpose, just to sense what that feels like. Hit it too lightly for the same reason. Never up, never in, is an expression that we all have experienced firsthand, cursing ourselves in the process. "You had the line. Just hit it, Alice" (sorry, ladies, but it's what many guys say . . . still). You don't have to study putting physics. Just spend some time on a putting green, trying all sorts of permutations and combinations.

Finally, change your routine. If you've plumb-bobbed for a long time, ditch it. If you've lined up your putts from behind the ball, try it from behind the hole. You will see an entirely different perspective, a truer perspective perhaps. Feel the green with your feet to get a sense of the break. Take the ocean or the mountains or the heavy guy you're playing with, into consideration. Check the course's stimp rating on their website. Anything ten or over is fast, so on downhill putts, just get the ball rolling, and let gravity be your friend. (The stimp is measured by rolling the ball down a little sliding board device, and seeing how far it rolls.)

Experiment. Find your own truth about putting—the truth that's found at the bottom of a cup and that lovely clicking sound the ball makes falling into it.

Zen Putting

In my observations as a student of the game, I have deduced that the older we get, the less adept we are in reading greens. This, of course, doesn't always hold true, but witness Tiger Woods, Steve Stricker, Vijay Singh, Davis Love III, John Daly, and other pros in their late thirties, forties, and fifties. Their strokes seem solid and true enough, but they are missing putts that they used to make routinely. Woods is the most graphic case of the bunch. Arguably, the greatest reader of greens in the history of the game may not have it anymore. And contrary to Johnny Miller's predictions, I don't think he's likely to get it back like he putted in his prime. Woods never missed from three to five feet, and from farther out, he was the best clutch putter on tour. No more. He's still good, compared to some other guys, but at best, he's slightly above average. Stricker, once considered the best putter on tour, has faltered some, and lost that razor-sharp precision. And Vijay, now mostly on the Champions Tour, hasn't won in several years, after a marvelous stretch in his early forties. Even John Daly, whose fluid, rhythmic stroke was the envy of many, still has that stroke but often can't find the line or the speed.

As for myself, I used to be a pretty darn good putter, helping me break 80 consistently years ago. I, too, still have a fluid stroke, keeping the head rock still; However, in my sixties, I just can't sink many putts, particularly the short ones for par and the fifteen footers for birdie, the way I used to. It's extremely frustrating after cozying up a decent chip or pitch to five feet (that's right: the chipping's not as good either) to miss a relatively easy putt for par. Demoralizing, really, and requiring a regrouping for the next hole, of which, in another sense, I am deeper in as per my ballooning score. With all the great equipment and help-ful instruction, I've never struck the ball better from tee to green, but I just can't read greens the way I used to in my younger days. I'm still good at reading the line of longer putts, by the way, of twenty-five feet and beyond, but my speed is often off by quite a bit. On the short ones, I have good speed but the line is off. Knowing this, is there any way to correct this disheartening situation?

To be honest, I'm still working on it, knowing more of what I should not do than what I should do. Back in the day, Palmer, Nicklaus, Casper, and Trevino were my models, for, despite their wristy tech-niques, those guys could read greens. Today, my models are McIlroy, Fowler, Snedeker, and Poulter, with Rory at the top of the list. First, they don't approach a putt like it was a coiled rattler. Older pro golf-ers, who've lost their keen ability to read putts, treat the putt like the approach-avoidance conflicts I studied as a psych major in college, often in doubt from start to finish, never quite committed to the line and speed as they crouch down, get up, walk around, get down again, stand over, back off, call in their caddy surgeons for a second opinion, replace the ball and pull their coin, stand over and address the ball, turn their eyes to the hole a few times, and . . . back away again, à la Jim Furyk or Ben Crane. First off, Rory enters the green after his approach like Robert the Bruce advancing into battle. He's reading the putt as he strides, getting a feel for the lay of the land, perhaps through his feet and certainly his eyes. He'll acknowledge the crowd's cheers, but, believe me, he's got that putt foremost in his mind.

With no other shot in golf is the mind any more important. Even an ounce of insecurity, one negative thought, a slight moment of doubt, will send infinitesimal twitches from the brain's neuronal net-work to the synaptic nerves endings in the hands and fingers, raising the ugly head of indecision as the golfer stands over the putt. The origin of the yips, defined. With Rory, you don't see this indecision much. Once he places his putter blade behind the ball, he pulls the trigger and sends the putt on its way. It's as much a Zen act of golf as I've ever seen. There is no fear in his stroke, and little indication of regret after he completes it. His mind, his body, his hands, his fingers, his eyes, are all working in unison. And he doesn't take a lot of time getting to this place before he putts. Again, he reads the battlefield green like a confident general, deciding where to strike, often without his caddy's input, and sticking to it, come hell or high water. That's key: wherever the ball winds up, his goal is to strike the putt solidly on the sweet spot. This is where his hearing enters the fray. As in tee to green shots, he wants to hear that certain click telling him that he's made pure contact with the putter. Yes, he wants to be aligned correctly. Yes, he wants to keep the head and neck still. Yes, he wants his eyes directly over the ball. Yes, he wants to minimize the movement of his wrists, making it more an arm and shoulder motion. Yes, he wants to pick a spot, over which he intends to roll the ball. But mainly, he wants to hear that magic click that tells him he's done all the above antecedents correctly.

Poulter, Fowler, and Snedeker all have similar approaches to the putting game, for it is truly a game within the game of golf. As Davy Crockett, the great American frontiersman and legislator, and a boyhood hero of mine, once said, "When you know you are right, go ahead." No doubt. No fidgeting. No thinking. No backtracking. No fretting. Size up the putt from as many angles as you want. Decide on your line and how far back you'll draw your blade or mallet. And stroke the bloody ball. Come hell or high water. No guarantees, except that you'll know you've hit your target cleanly and solidly. The true target? The ball against the putter's sweet spot.

HOLE 10
Swinging

SWINGING THE BODY was a joyous activity that we left behind long ago in childhood. But golf affords the opportunity to let go and swing again, in a more controlled way, true, but swinging it is. The mindful golfer puts the fun back in fundamentals through the freedom of swinging.

For many, though, as the line of golfers at a driving range will attest, swinging does not come easily. Adults are often self-conscious, stiff, out of shape. Golfing adults are apt to slip back into a comfort zone that does not always produce the most efficient golf swing. Adults, regrettably, think too much.

The Drive: A Journey to Better

I have struggled with the driver since I took up the game as a teenager many years ago. I never really learned how to control the longest club in the bag. I envied the number one player on my high school team, Henry Leon, for his driving ability. Henry was a fine all-around player and his driving was most impressive. A thin, wiry fellow, who had a Ben Hogan quality to him, Henry bristled with confidence, trusting his swing would set him up well to par or birdie any given hole. I, on

the other hand, never really trusted my tee ball swing, having to count on decent iron play and superior chipping and putting to land me the number two spot on the team and score consistently in the high 70s, low 80s. I was a good athlete but for some reason could not square up that persimmon head at impact. And today, I'm still struggling. I have my good days, but most often my driving is inconsistent and unpredictable. And driving, I believe, is the most important key to playing successful and satisfying golf. Driving is what defines golf as a sport and not just a game. When Rory McIlroy routinely smashes 330-yard drives down the fairway, fans take note.

There is nothing in sport quite like a well-hit drive. You want to hold that finish forever. You want to relive the feel of solidity as the ball springs from the clubface. You want to remember the sight of the ball soaring, landing, and rolling out on the fairway to a distance you know will set you up perfectly for your next shot. The drive should be a relatively easy shot. After all, the teeing ground is level, well manicured, mostly unobstructed by trees or bunkers straight ahead, and we can tee the ball up to whatever height we'd like: the perfect lie. There are fewer variables than any other shot in golf. The club is longer than any other, with the potential for the greatest clubhead speed in the bag. This should all add up to good distance and accuracy. At times, it does, but not enough times. I often lose five or six strokes per round from bad drives on a tree-lined golf course, which is the difference between being sentenced to the mid-80s and busting through to the 70s.

I've done extensive analysis of my swing and have come up with various theories on why I can't hit the damn club consistently well. My golfing buddy Steve was asking me the same question after our round the other day. "You hit your irons so well," he said. "Why not the driver?" Whereupon, he launched into a critique of my swing, concluding that I am standing too far from the ball at address. Could it be that simple? Probably not. The golf swing is a complicated array of movements and muscles and nerve cells, all of which have to be operating in coordination and correct rhythm and timing. I am 6'1, 180 lbs, am fairly strong and athletic, but can only hit the ball about 210 yards on average, occasionally reaching 230. That's frustrating, and that's a long iron or hybrid into many par 4's. It's not fun, and honestly, it's a bit embarrassing, especially when I tell people I've been playing this game for about fifty years. Of course, I *am* sixty-nine, and the swing and body *do* slow down, but my mind still wants to belt the ball a ton. Maybe it's a guy thing. We're hardwired to think "distance" no matter what age or body condition. We're hardwired to observe the other guy and want to knock it past him. We're competitive, and, you know, it's nothing to be ashamed of. I say, be true to your self, and *be* competitive, but with golf, that's not enough.

You have to be smart, too. You have to be patient. You have to hold back about 20 percent. You have to make good, solid contact, and sometimes the way to achieve that is to swing easier. I discovered that taking lessons a few years ago. The instructor had me take half swings and whaddyaknow, I was knocking it 150 yards down the middle with practically a bunt swing. Of course, when I started letting it out again, I was back in the trees, in trouble.

So, as I am wont to do, I started to think it was mental, that I had a block about this club. It was just a matter of confidence. Just swing it like a 7-iron. Tee it low. Or high. Or don't tee it at all. That's right: At one point, I garaged my driver, trying to hit 3-wood off the turf, no tee. I thought I might be tee phobic! Didn't work. None of it worked. I'd occasionally smack it out there, my confidence heightened. But then my hands would come over the top and I'd hit some miserable excuse for a golf shot, and my ego would be crushed. I was suffering a form of Charles Barkleyism, better known as the driving yips. (Although a tremendous athlete, Barkley is known for having an awkward swing, which many attribute to the yips.)

I do have a good driving round on occasion, so I know I have it in me. I do better, for example, on a course without trees—a links-type course. That's good to know, since it keeps me searching for the right formula, the right swing thoughts, the right mind set. Lately, I've been encouraged with my experiments. I'm moving in the right direction and feel that I'm advancing, albeit two steps forward, one step back, on the Holy Grail of driving.

The Drive: Hit it Hard

Doing a jigsaw puzzle can take a long time with many pieces to fit together. Such is the swing that motors the drive, and most all the other shots in golf. I've studied many books, apps, DVDs, and YouTube videos on the subject. I've observed the swings of PGA pros on tour, taping tournaments and watching in slow motion. I've tuned into dozens of instructional shows on the Golf Channel. I've spent hundreds on lessons. And I've devoured countless tips from golf magazines and online. And yet the jigsaw puzzle of driving a golf ball, for me, remained unsolved . . . until now.

The three main elements of the puzzle involve distance, accuracy, and consistency. Confidence will follow as a result, and will build with continued success. Everyone has their own puzzle to put together, and putting it together involves persistence, determination, patience, trust, grit, courage, the ability to learn from mistakes, the ability to get up after you've been knocked down, remembering what you've learned, applying the same fundamentals time after time, having the passion and pride to want to throw the bloody driver away, and the wisdom and restraint not to.

Here's my advice: hit it hard. Hit it as hard as you can and still stay in balance at the finish. Grip the club as light as you can and still keep the club from twisting in your hands at impact. Keep your head relatively steady and behind the ball through impact. Take the hands as high as your body flexibility and your straight forward arm will allow to the top of the backswing. Then bring the clubhead down toward the ball, on an inside path, straightening the arms as you approach the impact zone. Keeping an eye on the back of the ball, hit it hard. Then go find it. Where it goes will tell you where the clubface was pointing at impact. Make adjustments. Figure it out. If you pull it or slice it, you're coming over the top. If you push it, your ball position may be too much in the middle of your stance. If you hit it fat, you're too slow in shifting your weight to the forward foot on the downswing. If you hit it thin, you may be chicken-winging your forward arm. Think of it as a free and natural swing. The arms will lead, the body will follow. Just swing the arms. Don't concern yourself with the hips and legs. They will follow suit in a natural fashion. I believe there is too much emphasis on the lower body in instructing amateurs to play this game. The practice it takes to get the sequence right is too daunting. And the loss of accuracy drives people away from the game. I know many more experienced players will disagree with me, but just concentrate on swinging the arms. The ball has a better chance of staying in the fairway, keeping more beginners in the game.

These are the pieces of the puzzle. It's not rocket science. Fourteen clubs, one swing, as Jack says. Once you get the 7-iron down, apply it to the rest. I believe a relatively speedy swing keeps thoughts to a minimum, but pace is a personal thing. Thoughts kill a golf swing. One swing thought is OK but be careful: allow in one more than one and many may follow. As Annika Sorenstam says, stand behind the ball and think through the shot in the *Thinking Box*. Then move up to the *Play Box*. Here, you execute the shot without any further thought. It certainly worked for Annika.

The most important elements of this swing are to complete the backswing and extend the arms through the impact zone. A complete backswing happens when you have brought your hands to the height of your head with your left shoulder under your chin. Of course all this is knowledge from personal experience. I've taught golf from time to time, but I am not a PGA pro. I am a long-time student of the game, though. And I *am* a good teacher. But rather than believe me or not, based on my credentials or lack thereof, go and try it out. Experiment. And if you do figure it out, follow the advice of a banner strung across the entrance to a meditation hall I know: it simply says,

"Remember." Write down the procedures that work for you. Study them. Go apply them on the course. No one has written the final instructions on how to play this game.

There are no shortcuts to this great game. Go out and find your swing.

Align-iron-ment

Irons are a puzzle to many golfers. After all, in simple terms, you have to hit down on the ball to make it rise up. Loft is built into the club so it is not necessary to help it by scooping the ball into the air. Women, who are generally much neater and fastidious than men, have a particular problem with the action of irons since the clubs, when struck properly, take a divot in the turf, creating a messy result. But inexperienced male golfers, too, have a tough time with the concept. As with many aspects of golf, it's the mind that misunderstands what's required. Golf can be contra-intuitive.

To add to the confusion, not only do you need to hit down on the ball to make it rise, you have to align your shoulders, hips, and legs left of the target to hit the ball straight at the target, which is usually the flagstick on the green. Stay with me now. First, you point the clubface at the target, then you align the body left of the target, which telegraphs vital information, which the brain relays to the body to swing the club at the target. Got that? No? Don't feel bad. It took me about forty years to get it down, and I still forget the concept at times. Two sets of railroad tracks side by side: the clubface and the body (there are very simple, and inexpensive, alignment rods, available at golf shops, to help you graphically see and experience this). You do this with woods as well, but you have a bit more margin of error with those long clubs. With irons, any miscalculation, ergo misalignment, and you probably will miss the green, which you don't want to do. Witness Scotsman and Hall of Famer Colin Montgomerie, ever the Majors bridesmaid, with his 6-iron to the eighteenth green in the U.S. Open in 2006. He needed a par to win but pushed the shot right into the deep rough off the green, made bogey, and lost perhaps his best chance to win a major. Witness Phil Mickelson at the same Open, on the same hole, needing a par to win, or a bogey to tie, misaligning three horrid shots in a row to a double bogey, handing the treasured Open, the only major he hasn't won, to Aussie Geoff Ogilvy.

What's difficult for most golfers to understand is that the mind translates any misalignment of the body into an action that compensates and corrects for the misalignment. It's like when your tires are out of alignment: your car will automatically veer off course in response to the faulty alignment. It will also wear down your tires more, leading to further problems down the road. So, if your body is lined up right of target with the clubhead at the target, your hands will likely come over the top on the downswing, pulling the ball left, or slicing it to the right. If your body is lined up left of target with the clubhead at the target, your hands will leave the clubface open at impact, pushing the ball to the right. Either way, the ball will likely not head toward the target, unless you've made some goofy compensation that corrects it all at impact. We've all seen that swing and wonder how the guy does it. Fact is, he doesn't . . . consistently. Believe me, goofy compensations are no way to play this game.

So that's why the golf magazines use so much print space on alignment but still leave golfers scratching their heads. Then on top of that, they try to explain how to intentionally draw or fade the ball, which is integrally linked to alignment, and how you're not a real golfer until you can pull this off. I think Johnny Miller said that. Keep breathing: I'm not going to get into that here. Bending the ball is useful with a tree in front of you, but first you have to hit it straight consistently before you move onto advanced techniques.

So the amazing mind/brain complex knows where the body and club are pointing and red lights start flashing deep in the folds of the brain if they are at odds. It then sends messages—very, very fast messages—via nerve endings to muscles controlling the path of the swing. Those muscles then make adjustments as a computer program might when you misspell a word when it corrects the mistake in a split second. There are some words, though, that are spelled the same but have different meanings, and that's where a problem arises in grammar as well as golf. In grammar, those words are called homonyms and can get you in trouble with a thesis or term paper. In golf, it's a slice, a push, a pull, or a pull hook, which can get you in trouble if you're Jimmy Furyk and you come to the par 5, 16th at the 2012 U.S. Open at Olympic tied for the lead on the final day and you misalign your 3-wood tee ball trying to cut off a dogleg left and you overcook it into the garbage too far left (Arnold Palmer did the same thing, on the same hole, to blow the '66 Open!). Bogey. And the Open is gone. Furyk, I suspect, jolts up, wide-eyed, at three in the morning over that misalignment. Unlike Phil, though, at least he's already won an Open.

In that way, the results of misalignments are shocking, causing the equivalent of PTSD in golf. Of course PTSD in golf in no way compares to this malady in relation to the serious mental condition brought on by war, phobia, and childhood abuse. As a mental health counselor, I've worked with many people, over the years, with PTSD. It's a mind/body problem where the mind is traumatized by an unexpected event, causing an extreme physical reaction, which, in turn, causes another emotional event, often an anxiety attack. The memory of this then gets embedded in the brain's memory system and stays there for years, often needing therapy and/or medication to ameliorate. As I said, the results in golf are nowhere near as dire, but when a poor shot comes out of apparent nowhere, there is a sense of shock and, indeed, we fear it could happen again without an inkling of warning.

So go now, with courage, out to the links, and swing, with confidence and freedom, watching the ball sail to the target, knowing you will execute each shot properly aligned.

Chipping: Up and Down Re-found

For an amateur, good chipping may well be the best way to lower a handicap. And yet, despite how easy it looks, it remains one of the most difficult parts of the game. The reason for that is our persistent and intractable memory. If you've ever chili-dipped or skulled a chip you know what I mean. It's the most embarrassing and exasperating mis-hit in golf, as Hunter Mahan experienced on his last hole against Graeme McDowell at the 2010 Ryder Cup. Mahan flubbed a chip just off the green to lose the match, crying in shame at the press conference afterward. But even in a friendly foursome, we've all been there, wanting to break the club over our knee, as our playing partners stand nearby in silence—one of the most deafening silences in the universe.

What makes this shot so difficult? How can we do better? Arguably, it is the shot most affected by the mind. To strike the ball at such a slow pace gives the mind time to think and remember, and what it remembers is often the worst of what we've done in the past not the best. So we often approach the shot with an image of failure and apprehension. Tension enters the body via thought signals. And tension interrupts the flow and rhythm of the stroke.

I was a great chipper when I was a teen and shot in the 70s regularly. I had great confidence and could get up and down for par from virtually anywhere. I used anything from a 5-iron to a wedge, with a 7-iron being my favorite weapon of choice. Eventually life interceded, I played much less golf, and I lost my chipping touch, trying in vain to regain that feel and stroke for the next forty years, until recently . . . eureka! I rediscovered how to chip, and regained my confidence. Now, although I still misjudge the speed of the shot at times, I rarely mis-stroke the hit.

What I discovered was that I had changed my technique by buying into the modern method of keeping the hands, wrists, and arms quiet and moving only the shoulders. I remembered that when I was a kid, I modeled my short game after Arnold Palmer who was my inspiration to take up the game. He had a wristy, handsy short game, as did Billy Casper and other great pros of the day, which was markedly different from today's pros. So I began experimenting with this, along with a faster pace to the shot, and found I could hit the ball much more crisply and solidly. So I broke my wrists some on as short a backswing as possible, but, like today's pros, kept the hands ahead of the clubhead on the through swing. I play the ball off my back toe. The clubhead remains square to the target through impact and remains square in the short follow through.

The results were remarkable. Few thin or fat shots, and many more tap-in pars. The key, I think, is in the wristy, quick backswing, which more fits the sensitive nature of this shot. It's a feel shot, requiring absolute conviction at every phase. If one negative thought enters, the shot's death rattle begins, and memories of failure arise. The human brain is, perhaps, the most remarkable mechanism in the universe. It can bring balance to the organism or chaos. It's your choice.

I'm not suggesting you adopt my method. I came to it by remembering a past technique that once worked for me. I *am* suggesting you put more time into chipping practice than any other aspect of the game. Find a chipping practice area that allows you to practice various shots that arise and keep at it until something clicks and you start to hit shots that feel solid, that are true chips that rise initially then hit the green in the right spot and run the rest of the way to the hole. Unfortunately, perhaps because they generate no income, chipping areas are often woefully inadequate, too small and poorly designed to accommodate a decent practice session. Good ones are out there, though, so keep looking until you find one.

Perfect Pitch

For the first time in my golf life, I got clear on the distinction between the pitch and the chip, and the definition and use of bounce. This revelation came after watching Paul Azinger teach a short game clinic hosted by Brandel Chamblee on Golf Channel. The chip, explained Azinger, is a shot off the green where you have enough green to land the ball just on and let it run the rest of the way. Weight is on the forward foot, the shaft leans forward, the forward edge of the face is slightly hooded, the ball is played off the back big toe, the hands are ahead of the ball at impact, striking the ball first, and any manner of club is used from wedge to hybrid. There is some wrist action going back, with the arms and hands leading the way going forward into impact—a relatively simple shot if performed correctly. But if your ball lands farther off the green after your approach, which is the case for many amateurs, the pitch is the appropriate shot, and good execution can save many strokes.

Now the idea for most shots near the green is to land the ball on the green and let it run to the hole. If you are in pitch range, though, and try to chip it with a consequent lower trajectory, the ball may land in the fringe before the green and be subject to the inconsistencies of that terrain. Therefore there's a greater tendency for the ball to be knocked off line, or even stopped by the longer fringe grass. That has to be one of the most frustrating shots in golf when you've done well to get close to the green, only to have the fringe gobble up and waste a shot with a chip that should have been a pitch. So what is a pitch? How is it played? And what in the Sam Hill *is* bounce anyway?

Bounce is the meaty, rounded protuberance behind the face, at the bottom of iron clubs. The greater the loft of the club, the more the bounce. So the sixty-degree wedge has more bounce than the pitching wedge, which has more bounce than the 7-iron. Woods and hybrids have no bounce. Of course, a wedge can have more or less bounce depending on the manufacturer or club fitter. With a pitch shot, bounce is your friend. Why is it called bounce? Because what you don't want is the forward edge of the club taking a big divot. You want the club to "bounce" off the turf just behind and under the ball.

That is because bounce, if the club is swung properly, will increase the trajectory of the ball, allowing it to land on the green first and not the fringe. If executed right you can land that pill a couple feet from the hole, have it release a tad, and make it stop like a hummingbird on a sweet flower. Ergo, a tap-in next shot. This is definitely one of the most satisfying shots in golf, and will have your buds asking, "How did you do that?"

Now you may have marveled when you've seen a pro who's flown a green, short-side himself into thick rough, take this huge backswing and short follow through, flying the ball about a foot or two, and having it trickle to the hole à la Phil. Amazing shot, isn't it? Well, it was bounce that got him there. And, as my friend Rob Wallace says, it was courage as well. Because if you have any doubt or hesitation, you could easily hit this shot fifty feet over the green, or maybe your playing partner's noggin as she stands on the green waiting to putt. But the way to pull off this shot, Azinger-style, is not often taught by modern instructors because they probably don't want to be embarrassed when trying to demonstrate it. First, keep the feet close together, slightly open to the target. Weight is evenly distributed, if anything favoring the right side rather than the left (yes, you read that correctly). The shaft of the club is perpendicular to the body, ninety degrees, with the hands opposite the navel. Use a high-lofted club with plenty of bounce. Using arms and some wrist action, employ a fairly long backswing, the length of which depending more on the distance to the hole, not to the green. At impact, the coup de grace is slightly behind the ball without taking much of a divot, which the bounce prevents. Of course, this shot becomes ever more challenging with a tight lie as opposed to having some grass under the ball. In fact, Zinger likes the ball to be in the first cut of rough so he can sweep under it, a bit like he would a bunker explosion. On a tight lie you have to nip it just right to get the bounce to do its job. Tough assignment, but not impossible. As an aside, this shot is not advisable on most links courses, like St. Andrews or Pacific Dunes, where a putter would be your best and safest tool to get it close to the hole. The fringe and fairways on these layouts are not that much different than the greens on parkland courses.

The follow through is much shorter than the backswing, but you must not decelerate into impact. That's where courage comes in. And if done properly, the ball floats off the clubface like a badminton birdie, perhaps leading to a golf birdie. The key to this shot is to get the ball to land near the hole, because you won't get much roll. And, for this, much practice is needed. Just make sure there aren't buildings with windows, or other golfers, in your line, because thin mis-hits could be disastrous. And fat mis-hits have their own problems. Try it first with grass under your ball, and when you get good at it, advance on to tighter lies.

But to get it right, you need to make the right decisions about the shot. First, can you chip it? The margin of error for a chip is much greater, so if you can chip it, do so. Second, which club to pick? A 60 will land and roll less than a 56, a 56 less than a 52, and so on. So use the least lofted club possible for the pitch, since that will increase your margin of error. In golf you always want as much margin of error as possible on all shots. Risk/reward is fine but be smart about it, always rigorously subjecting your decisions to reality testing. And finally, make sure your lie offers you a decent chance to pull this shot off. The tighter the lie, the less you should attempt this shot, unless you've practiced it big time.

It's a challenge, but the pitch is, arguably, one of the greatest scoring shots in all of golf. Try it. Find a spot you can safely practice it. It may change your entire perspective on the game, increasing your fun factor, amazing your friends, and lowering your handicap like no other aspect of this demanding game.

Course Management

So you're standing on the tee, gazing out at the challenge ahead, thinking you have several options for the next shot. There's a creek running across the fairway about 210 yards, definitely in range of your tee ball. There are trees on the left, and a fairway bunker down the right side, also within range of your normal distance off the tee with a driver. You've played eight holes, three in par, four in bogey, and one in double bogey. This hole is a relatively short par 4, but that creek is a question mark. The fairway is dry and the ball is running considerably. You're hitting your driver fairly well on this day. How to play this hole? This is the essence of course management. From the time you approach the tee box, you have about two minutes to make all these decisions. Of course, as amateurs, your only goal at this point is to place the ball in the fairway, anywhere in the fairway, and not in the creek or the trees or the bunker. Strategy becomes more specific the closer we get to the hole. But still, we know we're capable of reaching that creek so it sticks in the mind like a jumping cholla. We choose a 3-wood and let 'er rip.

Course management involves knowing your game and what you're capable of. It also involves the ego, that part of the self that is so full of itself, it makes decisions that are often completely unrealistic, given past performance. Animals supposedly don't have egos, so predicting their behavior is relatively easy. They act in rote ways, traveling similar routes and reacting similarly regardless of external factors. That's why a lot of wildlife get hit by cars. Roads cross regular migration routes, and animals know only one way to get to their destination. People, though, make choices based on the needs and desires of their egos. And as soon as you bring other options into play, you enter unknown territory and the consequences of risk-reward scenarios. Like, for example, the couple with a baby who decides to take an old shortcut across the Sierras in a snowstorm with a quarter tank of gas and no cell phone. The only survivor was the baby.

Virtually every shot has within it some risk-reward factor. Should I risk going over that bunker to get closer to a tucked away pin in the back of the green? The closer I get to that creek, the closer to the green and the shorter the club I'll need to get there. If I can keep it low and under those tree branches, I can reach the green and save par. I can reach this par 5 in two, if only I can clear the pond in front of the green. Each of those situations involves risk, which can lead to reward or punishment, success or failure, agony or ecstasy. If the ego is in charge, without any restraint, it will think only of the rewards and take on the risk. Examples would be Arnold Palmer, Seve Ballesteros, and Phil Mickelson—all of whom were/are great golfers but who came up a bit short of their potential in relation to major tournaments won. The U.S. Open is perhaps the best example of a tournament that punishes too much risk taking. Palmer won in 1960, but never again, and the other two never won an Open. Seve was a swashbuckler who got up and down from parking lots. And who could forget Phil the Thrill blowing the '06 Open with a double bogey from behind the trees on the seventy-second hole. Arnie, Seve, and Phil thought they could make any given golf shot. They all had/ have egos that encouraged too much risk taking. They had the skills that led to many rewards, but, like Babe Ruth, they led the league in strikeouts as well.

The way to keep the ego in check and make good course management decisions is to "know thy golf game." Know how far you hit each club. Know how you're playing on any given day. Know your distances to bunkers, creeks, and greens. Know the course you're playing, what's hidden over that hill, how much green you have to work with. Know not only the distance but how much height will it take to clear that tree and reach the green. Information. For, after all, golf is a thinking person's game. Ironic, isn't it? Golf requires much thinking so you can ultimately clear the mind and swing with the enlightened grace of a mindless Aikido sensei.

Of course, keeping the ego in check is no easy matter. Buddhism was built upon doing so, and after 2,500 years still struggles with the egos of its students. It took the author Carlos Castaneda years before he began to understand the path of enlightenment that his teacher Don Juan painstakingly showed him, always encouraging him to put down his pen and pad and experience life as it is. And Jesus, and Joan of Arc, and Martin Luther King Jr. went to their deaths rather than compromise their state of selflessness. It takes courage to let go of the influence of ego. You need to be determined to do so. You need to have strong intent to do so. You need to resolve to identify the telltale signs of ego, hold them up to the karmic light, and resist heeding them. The ego draws addicts to destructive behavior. It beckons con artists to steal. It walls out compassion. It deceives one into thinking he can do anything without consequence. I believe that if Tiger had his ego in check, he would have been wiser and made better decisions in his personal life.

The key is mindfulness and awareness. The crust of ego hardens through conditioning, but conditioning can be reversed. First, the ego and its henchmen must be observed and noticed. The ego depends on the shadows of one's self to do its work. It is like a criminal in the night, unseen, robbing freedom wherever possible. And once its ways are seen, it can be stopped in its tracks and replaced with more rational, less harmful, more conscious thoughts and actions. If you're behind a tree, stop before you attempt to slice the ball around the tree, and ask yourself, "Have I practiced this shot? Have I ever pulled it off before? If it doesn't slice, what further trouble will it lead to?" Thinking you can successfully pull off such a shot, for most players, is a barometer of ego gone wild. See it. Confront it. Put it down. Take your one-shot medicine and knock the ball back into the fairway, telling yourself it's just a game, and proceed with the hole without a thought of what just happened. In that instant you mounted a frontal attack against ego and won. All it cost was one shot to your score. Not a tough price to pay for helping to break the conditioned response of the ego—the part of the self that thinks it knows just about everything.

And don't stop there. Keep your level of awareness high and notice where ego raises its arrogant head. You now have a way to take away its power—a power you yourself give it through the shadows you create via non-awareness. What happened to the 3-wood and the creek on the short par 4? No problem with the creek but you're in the bunker. As a big number looms, more options to figure out . . . quickly.

Finding and Trusting your Rhythm

I'm not much of a dancer, but when I get out on the dance floor with my wife, I depend less on technique and mostly on my rhythm to get by. My parents, on the other hand, were champion ballroom dancers, employing both technique and rhythm to win titles (they were fine musicians too—my mother, a great pianist and singer, and my father, a percussionist who could even find rhythm in a washboard). In golf, technique is essential, but good rhythm seals the deal. And keeping good rhythm as the round progresses is one of the hardest elements of the game to maintain. The reason it's tough is that so many subtle things affect rhythm. There are the external elements like wind, heat, cold, rain, mud, and the big-bomber gorilla you're playing with. And there are the internal factors like concentration, focus, presentness, pain, and the rent check you forgot to send off. Of course good technique is vital, but without good rhythm, good technique alone won't cut it. And with good rhythm, bad technique won't either. For technique, follow some of the suggestions in this book, or see a PGA pro for lessons. For rhythm, pick the club you're most comfortable with, probably a short iron, and swing all your clubs like you swing that one.

Now that's not as easy as you think, because the tendency is to increase the pace of the swing as the clubs get longer. The longer the shot, the harder, and most importantly, faster, we think we need to swing. It's a direct correlation: the longer the shot, the faster the swing; the shorter the shot, the slower the swing. The only problem is it doesn't work that way. Longer clubs are designed longer to increase the arc of the swing, and a wider arc increases the clubhead speed. Rhythm and pace stay the same for all clubs, resulting in one more element crucial for longer clubs: balance. Without balance, you can't stay in control of the longer clubs, which are apt to throw you more off balance than the shorter ones.

Hitting into a stiff breeze is perhaps one of the best examples of why it's important to swing within ourselves. I've experimented with this and found that the tendency is to swing faster into the wind. Not only is balance affected and the shot can easily go astray, but even on solid hits a harder swing often leads to higher shots that balloon into the wind. The antidote is to swing at the pace of a short iron, and shorten the follow through so as to cut down clubhead speed. A low bullet results (good also for keeping it low under tree branches).

Achieving this kind of pace and rhythm in playing conditions is about as easy as wrestling an alligator. Even touring pros struggle with it. I was watching the European Tour from Morocco and seeing how each of the three contenders lost their rhythm in the maelstrom of competition and pressure. Each one crumbled, causing forced errors that showed they were out of the present moment. Rhythm is most affected by the mind and where its focus is or isn't in any given moment. The mind must be trained to stay with the task at hand. Phil Mickelson admitted in an interview that the reason he had not done well a few years ago was he had not been able to maintain his concentration throughout four rounds of competitive golf. He had a lot on his mind, between his own arthritic condition, and his wife's and mother in law's battles with cancer.

But for amateurs like you and me, who don't have the time to practice and consult coaches on a daily basis, the best approach is to train the mind to fight those alligators. I would suggest two things, one on the range and one in your living room. First take three clubs with you to your next practice session: a 7-iron, a hybrid, and a driver. First hit your 7-iron ten times at your normal pace. Then hit your hybrid at the same pace as your 7-iron, then hit your driver ten times at the same pace as your hybrid. Your aim is to make solid contact with all three clubs, especially the driver, which is the toughest club to hit consistently. I guarantee that driver will go farther and straighter than usual.

Second, go to your favorite chair in your living room. Find a quiet time of day. Relax in your chair, both feet on the floor, hands folded in your lap. Close your eyes, and bring your attention to the air going in and out of your nostrils or the rising and falling of your diaphragm. Just watch it for a few minutes. Let your thoughts settle like the precipitate in a test tube, leaving only clear liquid in the top of the tube— the tube in this case being your mind. Do this every day, if possible, or as much as you can. This is the ultimate "taking a breather." It will train your mind to be in the present and focused. It gives you a temporary break from thinking. It's called meditation. No mumbo jumbo. No mantras. No religious dogma. No problem. Just do it.

If you can increase the time you meditate, all the better. You will begin to see results on the golf course. You will hit more good shots, but you will also meet your poor shots with more equanimity. You will more maintain that 7-iron pace throughout the round. And, perhaps most importantly, you will be a more patient, tolerant, calm, compassionate, and focused person.

You win. The world wins. And it might even improve your dancing.

HOLE 11

On High

___

GOLF IS A competitive sport that pits the player more against the golf course than other players. Because there is no body contact with others, nor violence as we know it with other sports, there is the opportunity for more civility and higher consciousness in relation to others on the course. Mindful golf involves a heightened consideration for others—human and other species, offering a chance to practice a spiritual path while playing a fun game that goes back 600 years.

The other day, my buddy, Steve Prebble, did something unusual for a golfer: he bunted his ball down the fairway at Adobe Creek, wasting several strokes in the process, so as not to harm Canada geese who were feeding, willy-nilly, up ahead of his tee shot. Steve has done this with deer as well. Above all, he does not want to harm wildlife in the course of playing golf. That is an example of conscious, mindful golf.

Where Lions Lie with Lambs: The Golf Course

After the horrid tragedy of a madman killing school children in Newtown, Connecticut in 2013, I reflected on the few places left in our society where, for the most part, peace and calm reign supreme. The golf course is one such place, making me thankful to be a golfer.

Violence is rare on a golf course. Even verbal violence, brought on by discourtesy, is an aberration, short lived and relatively mild. The course, the driving range, are places I can go to relax, to unwind, to meditate, to have fun, to attain a goal without stepping over anyone, to practice a new theory, to get good at something in a quiet way, indeed, to be relatively quiet, away from the phone or tablet or table or desk, to be independent, to be in nature, to walk, to meet new people on a first name basis, whether a Senator, a doctor, a judge, a butcher, a baker, a social worker, or the Prince of Wales, or POTUS, and to high-five any of them after a chip-in birdie. Golf is one of the few activities left where etiquette is emphasized and actively taught through observation of other players. Most golfers are polite to one another. Most wait for the group in front of them to clear out of the way before they tee off. This is more out of consideration for the safety of others than from any rule. The golfer thinks, "I think I can reach those guys so I'll wait a bit more," as he calculates how far he can hit it in relation to where those people are in the fairway. That is a very conscious thing to do. It is a mindful thing to do. When you take another person, or sentient being of any kind, into account, that is a noble, mindful thing to do. It happens often on a golf course, any golf course, whether in the inner city or out in the country.

Now, there may be killers and criminals among golfers. There may be mean people who have nasty streaks, capable of road rage or spousal abuse or fraud. But there is something about golf and golf courses that soothes the savage beast within, something within the DNA of a golf course that transforms the golfer and encourages higher consciousness and consideration, that brings out the best in people. What is it about golf and its playing fields?

For one thing the playing of golf requires the synchronization of body and mind, making it unique among many modern activities. Often the mind and body are split, causing a dissonance within a human being, like a note sung off key. At the extreme, we have a madman killing children. But even to a much lesser extent, we have overly sensitive people getting annoyed or being rude or shoving to get to the head of the line or darting into traffic. Most people, at any given moment, are somewhat split between mind and body. It's endemic in modern society and causes a certain degree of disharmony. When a golfer approaches a golf ball, he or she focuses the mind on that ball and prepares the body to advance that ball in a favorable way. The mind and body, whether well prepared or not, are in unison, to varying degrees, yes, but more together than most people in the world off the golf course. Most others are doing one thing while thinking of something entirely different. Golf demands a certain presentness, a certain concentration, a certain intention that gathers the mind and body in a crescendo that culminates in the impact zone. Regardless of the result, whether it is slice or hook or shank, every golfer reaches that crescendo where mind and body have succeeded in making impact with the ball. That, in itself, is an extremely calming moment, leaving no room for thoughts of disharmony, violence, harmfulness, revenge, anger, or any other negative tendency. Now those thoughts and feelings might arise after experiencing the results of the shot, but at impact, before the results are known, body and mind are unified and at peace in that particular moment. Golfers are often in this moment of impact during a round or on the range, these moments of mindfulness and catharsis, which soothe and calm the human spirit.

The golf course, alone, is another important factor in this feeling of harmony. All courses are crafted and carved from nature, and nature is the perfect example of harmony and balance in action. If left to itself, nature grows, sometimes even more so after natural disaster. Native Americans knew that and were our last residents to live in relative harmony with their natural surroundings. So, in the twenty-first century, spending time in a place of nature is bound to trigger memories of when humans lived closely to Mother Earth. Today, we are mostly cut off from the natural environment—the smell of bark, the sound of birds, the instability of mud, the fragrance of spring, a drizzle on our face, the sight of a pillowed cloud on a hot summer day. Instead we are at our desks, in our cars, at the mall, in line at the DMV, at the supermarket. Nature? What? Where? Why? On the golf course, even if we're tooling around in a motorized cart, we are experiencing more nature than most, and even if we're not aware of it, we are being healed as a result.

That's right, nature is such that our bodies, our minds, our very souls, are taking in its effects even if we are not aware of it. At the core, we are one with nature, and some part of us is aware of that, even if unconscious. Of course the more aware you are of that fact, the more mindful you can become. But even if just one of your cells is aware of its connection with nature, the whole is equal to the sum of its parts, and you are on the road to a deeper mindfulness. We are very sensitive beings, we humans, and the more time we spend in nature, the more harmony we feel. And that is an important reason golf courses are peaceful places. They encourage us to leave our cars parked for a while and return to our roots.

Higher Golf Consciousness

At the Nature Valley First Tee Open at Pebble Beach, Champions Tour players match up with First Tee kids from around the country. It's a benefit for this fabulous organization that teaches kids not only how to play but the core values that golf represents. I was touched hearing one young man's story of his struggles with addiction and how golf and the First Tee helped lift him out of the ashes and into self-respect and hope. His parents were also interviewed later, and a look of pride and gratitude radiated from their faces. Pro Olin Browne stood next to the boy during their round, congratulating him for his courage and fortitude, and for the birdie on the last hole.

Golf values? First Tee participants learn to appreciate diversity, resolve conflicts, build confidence and set goals for their future. Its life skills curriculum focuses on four categories—interpersonal skills, self-management, goal-setting, and resilience skills and nine core values—honesty, integrity, sportsmanship, respect, confidence, responsibility, perseverance, courtesy, and judgment. I wish there was a First Tee for adults, something like a Second Chance Tee. Golf needs such a makeover. The game has slipped both quantitatively and qualitatively: Fewer people are playing the game, and of those who do play, there is less courtesy, honesty, integrity, and respect. There is less consciousness, a word not widely used or understood in our often-egocentric society. Since the end of World War II, we have become the "me-my-mine" generation, and that includes all age groups. Golf's bar of civility has been lowered, evidenced by pros spitting on putting greens, being dismissive of fans, fans being disrespectful to pros by snapping their photos and yelling "Get in the hole!" or even crazy stuff like "mashed potatoes!" dangerously close to impact. Amateurs plod along like armadillos, oblivious to the needs of others, encrusted with that ego mentality that slows things to a stop, making it near impossible to maintain any semblance of rhythm and pace in one's swing. And it doesn't seem to matter whether someone is experienced or a hacker. The experienced have deluded themselves into believing their money games take precedence over anyone else's game, leading them to line up putts like the interminable touring pro Ben Crane, causing approaching players to consider either *harakiri,* homicide, or giving up the game entirely. Consciousness is a fragile evolutionary trait, and the actions of one player can help tip the scales one way or the other. It's like the hundredth monkey concept, where monkeys on one Pacific island began washing their potatoes, which then led monkeys on other islands to do the same even though they had no contact with the first potato-washing monkeys. Get it? Start being conscious yourself and other golfers will catch on and increase their own consciousness.

And what exactly is consciousness? It's a sine qua non for all the values of the First Tee. Simply said, it is taking into account the condition of others, whether animal, vegetable, or mineral. And once taken into account, it is acting in a way that will protect, benefit, and enhance the lives of others while taking care of oneself at the same time. Even more simply said, consciousness is the Golden Rule: do unto others as you would have them do unto you. Let's be clear. We have often distorted that rule to read, do unto others as you think they would do unto you. It's a trick of our often distrusting, almost paranoid minds to ignore the needs of others because you think they don't give a damn about you. That's what we're devolving into, and that has to change.

And if we can change into more conscious beings, we open up the possibility of reaching the tipping point, a concept proposed by Malcolm Gladwell in a book of the same name. It's a point that's reached when a trend or preference of a few goes viral and inhabits the consciousness and actions of the many. It can start with something very small, like a few people wearing flip flops to something very big, like millions around the world wearing this unlikely footwear. It can be a word like "cool" or "like," or some tinkering in a garage in Palo Alto into a company called Apple.

So how do we increase our consciousness as golfers? Let's start with small things—things that get us to pay attention to those around us. Things that get us out of our own limited sense of self and into considering the needs of others. I'll list some.

- Be careful not to step in the line of a playing partner's putt. Again, apply the Golden Rule.
- Don't talk, move, or stand in a peripheral visual line when others are swinging. Golf requires intense concentration. Any distraction detracts from that concentration.
- Keep up. Always monitor your own pace of play by checking your position in relation to the group in front and the group behind you. Forget about traipsing the woods looking for a worn-out ball.
- Leave the pot, beer, and cigars at home. The only high on a golf course should be the high-five after a great shot. To be more conscious of others, stay sober and smoke free.
- Tend the flagstick, with your shadow out of the way, for others who may need it.
- Yell "fore" if your ball is flying near another golfer. And don't hold back. Yell it loud. I was hit once in the upper back from a fairway wood without a peep from the ball striker. No fun there.

- Compliment good shots. It's a tough game. Golfers need support and encouragement.

Of course, there are other factors, but this will get you started on the road to higher golf consciousness. You'll be helping to speed up play. You'll be known as a knowledgeable, courteous player, and you'll be sought out as a playing partner. I think, too, it will help improve your game. Being more conscious of others helps you be more conscious of yourself—your body, your mind, your swing, and your relationship to the moment at hand.

And support the First Tee. The future of this game depends upon it. The more conscious kids we can send out to the courses, the more healthy the future of this game becomes. Volunteer. Donate. Cheer them on at benefit tournaments. Arnold Palmer promotes it: So should you.

Developing Concentration: from Range to Course

I am a great driving range player. I have my off days, but for the most part I look like a pro on the range. In fact, people sometimes come up and compliment me on my swing, asking how I developed it. What I'm thankful for is that they usually don't follow that up inquiring about my handicap. For, as we well know, playing great on the range does not guarantee playing great on the course. The problem, I think, is physical and mental, perhaps even spiritual, when you consider the nebulous arena of concentration. At any rate, all of these factor into preparing to play the game of golf.

We get into a kind of mini-groove on the range. We get comfortable and relaxed. We get confident. The flat lies are nearly perfect. We are fresh and alert, and only need to reach over and rake another ball to the hitting area. Fatigue is a minor problem, a factor nearer to the end of the bucket. Unless you're practicing with a buddy, no one is talking to you between shots. Your concentration is solid. You are deep into golf meditation. You have your off days at the range. A personal problem may be distracting you. A physical problem may be the cause, throwing off your concentration. Still, it is easier to establish or regain concentration at the range than on the course.

Concentration is focusing on one thing at a time in such a way that all else is excluded from your attention in any given moment. Playing golf requires it every time a shot is played. In other words, golf does not demand concentration every moment you're on the course or the range, but it does when every shot is played. It is the moment when the one who experiences and that which is experienced meld into one powerful force, and the greater the concentration, the more powerful, and effective, the force.

So the way to translate your skill from the range to the course involves two things—improving and grooving your skills, and improving your concentration. One without the other won't do it. For grooving your swing, see a good pro and practice what he or she teaches. I like Hank Haney's advice to actor Ray Romano: just once, Hank told Ray on the Golf Channel, he'd like to hear Ray repeat some instruction he gave him instead of him telling Hank what he thinks he's doing wrong. Think of your pro as a swing guru: his word is gospel, and if you don't believe the word of that pro, look for someone else. You do not know everything that's wrong with your golf swing. You know where the ball goes after you hit it, and could describe that, although your pro has eyes too, very trained eyes. So just listen, and put into effect what your pro is telling you. Imagine yourself ten years old again and just learning the game. You will follow everything your pro tells you.

As for learning concentration, that is more of a challenge, for it is more a matter of eliminating elements from consciousness than adding anything, as one would do in the usual classroom or seminar. Demonstrating the extreme of concentration, the Buddhist meditator slowly peels away the skins of the onion on the journey to the core of his being. Worry not: a golfer doesn't have to go that deep, but the process is similar. You have to let go of that which has no relevance to the moment at hand. And when I say moment I mean that which is happening before you at that instant in time. It's easier to do this on the range simply because there are fewer stimuli to let go of. You get into a zone quite similar to a Buddhist meditation session, only instead of sitting on a cushion following your breath, you're standing in front of a golf ball, following the movements your body makes in striking that ball. If it goes well, you stay on that track. If it goes awry, you make changes, modifications, give mental instructions to your body, and change clubs. And you do this until you run out of balls or a time or fatigue limit comes into play. You even maintain the kind of silence one keeps during Buddhist meditation. So the mind quiets and grows more still. You forget about the D your kid got in math. You forget about the mortgage payment. You forget about your boss. You forget about the argument you had with your spouse. An hour has passed and, regardless of results, you have been extremely absorbed in one activity. It's a good feeling, isn't it? Taking it a few steps further, the Buddhist meditator knows it as absorption into the present moment.

So the range is a great place to experience and practice concentration. It won't necessarily be cumulative, but the more your mind gets to know what concentration is, the more comfortable it is with it and willing to return to that pleasant state. I think that's why golf is so addictive: concentration is an opiate, a really positive opiate.

So the trick then is not only to bring your swing knowledge and experience to the course from the range but also your concentration knowledge and experience. This is the next level of proficiency, and what touring pros mean when they say they're ready "to take my game to the next level." And the ability to focus and concentrate is really what separates the good and great pros. They can all shoot 65 on any given day, but then what happens the next day and the next? You have to raise your level of awareness around as many golf moments as possible. You have to isolate those moments on the course that are particularly important to your game. Part of that "next level" is coming to terms with having at least thirty-five balls and shots in front of you on the range, to having one ball and one shot at a time on the course.

That can be intimidating, stressful, and even anxiety producing, all of which can rob you of concentration.

To prevent that kind of internal robbery of a vital element of your golf game, you'll need to start with assessing your lie, checking your yardage, and choosing a club. Stay in the present moment by staying aware of the pace of your breathing. At that point of approaching a particular shot, social conversation stops and the concentration process begins. This pre-shot routine takes attention and making the right decisions. Pick a wrong club and you set yourself up for failure. Mis-analyze the lie and you're in trouble before you even swing. Read Jack Nicklaus's book *Golf My Way*, and you'll find out that even taking the proper grip and grip pressure takes close concentration and attention to details. Concentrate on one element of the pre-shot routine at a time, overlooking nothing, until you are over the ball ready to fire away.

Now you are deep into golfing meditation, actually doing much more than playing golf. It is not often that we are absorbed in an interesting activity during any given day. Such a state is good for the body, mind, and spirit. It's nourishing and refreshing. It reminds us that we are conscious human beings and we can direct that consciousness and intelligence wherever we wish. How often are you reminded of that in your life?

Now this is where the skills training on the range comes into play. A swing thought or two should put you on track to repeat what you practiced. This is why golf never developed a cheering crowd atmosphere like at the 16th at the Phoenix Open every year. The fans, who are often golfers, know what these guys are going through—from Old Tom Morris to Ricky Fowler, silence is a prerequisite to golf. The swing takes all of two to three seconds, but within that time you have to be at the height of that concentrative state. One stray or negative thought can obstruct the flow. The chain of silence breaks. But keep the concentration intact and you are transported into another realm, another level, of golf consciousness. You are in *Golf in the Kingdom*, where golf shots are made more in the mind than with the body.

One more thing that may help: just before you swing, take a standard waggle of the club, but let your body settle into stillness before you trigger the swing. Watch videos of Nicklaus: he's a master at this. Movement and fluidity, a moment of stillness, then fire away. That still head could be your final swing thought before swinging. But you pick what's best for you.

Where the ball goes almost doesn't matter. You have brought all the essential elements you developed at the range with you to the course and have executed well. Eventually as more focus hones the concentration process, you will think less about results while watching your results improve over time. This is true because when you've been able to keep not only your head steady but your mind still you will have entered the present moment, unconcerned with past, future, and even the present itself. That is total concentration, and that's when good things start to happen . . . when you're not even hoping for good things to happen. For the best of those good things is the feeling of being in that moment itself. Believe it or not, you may even feel happy after a "bad" shot—happy not for the shot but for the realization of being one of the fortunate few in this world who have the time, privilege, and resources to play golf at all.

So regardless of your level of proficiency, you keep trying. You keep practicing. And you keep taking a bit more from your instruction, a bit more from practice at the range, and a bit more from playing on the course. And keep a half smile on your face, as the Buddhists suggest, as this fascinating journey of golf, and life, continues.

Golf, as Pure Play, can Heal

Consider that golf spelled backward is flog, indicating that it can be punishing and, at times, painful. This may be why the game is not drawing the numbers of players it needs to stay healthy. But, unbeknownst to many, golf also heals. I have suffered, to varying degrees, emotional discontent throughout my life, but when playing golf, my unease disappears into the ether of play. It's a place where concerns of the day no longer plague me, as my mind and body are preoccupied with the demands of playing as good a game as I can. I imagine knitting would have the same effect, but golf adds the wind, sun, and the sound of birds to the mix, elements that help the healing by putting me in touch with this amazing planet we all occupy. It's a game that can transcend the ego, particularly when pure contact between club and ball is accomplished. And, unlike knitting, it offers a different challenge for each shot—a fact that focuses the mind, taking it away from personal troubles and into the healing realm of pure play.

Golfing is one of those times an adult can suspend responsibilities and just play. And play, often denied in the din of obligation, is good for the soul. Golf, perhaps more than any other game, involves so many of the senses that it forces the player to be absorbed in the present moment. And when one is so absorbed, healing can happen. The guards at the gates of the ego grow tired and fall asleep allowing the angels of play to enter and overwhelm its obsessions. For play is an antecedent of healing, softening a calcified ego that tightens the mind and tenses the body. Play requires no effort, no plan for accomplishment, no strategy. Observe a child and see the expert on play in action. Is there any more relaxed, involved human being than a child at pure play? Nothing to accomplish. Nowhere to go. Nothing really to do, since doing has little to do with play. Play comes naturally, a birthright of all beings.

And when pure play returns to your golf game, joy returns, reminding you of those feelings you experienced as a child. No matter what your score or how you did on your last shot, you can return to play by treating that next shot as your first of the round, full of hope and energy and vigor. If your mind will allow, golf offers the redemption of renewal with every shot. I saw this in pros I grew up watching like Arnold Palmer, Gary Player, Jack Nicklaus, Lee Trevino, Seve Ballesteros, and Tom Watson. And I see this today in pros like Keegan Bradley, Brandt Snedeker, Rory McIlroy, Graeme McDowell, Phil Mickelson, and, in his earlier days, Tiger Woods. No situation could intimidate these pros because they weren't playing golf: they were just playing. And the art of playing overcomes the vicissitudes of ego.

For ego breeds fear, its principal ally. Fear can serve a legitimate purpose like turning over your wallet to someone facing you with a gun. But fear has the pernicious habit of feeding on itself, eventually engorging the organism doing the digesting, namely you or I. When fear enters the nerve endings of a golfer, replacing the joy of play, the ensuing electrical impulses firing throughout the body play havoc with rhythm, timing, and a clear, unfettered mind, leading to tops, chunks, slices, shanks and other unmentionables, leading to thrown clubs, curses, mutterings, and other expressions the polar opposite to play. When a house of cards tumbles, kids usually chortle in delight.

So golf doesn't necessarily heal, but play does. How to put play back into golf is, ironically, not easy. Years of being an adult are often the source of that difficulty. Years of frustrated ambition, dashed expectations, and checkered results from being golfers jade us into not believing in ourselves. So we approach each shot with trepidation, with the thought of where not to hit it, or, worse, a vision of impending doom. The thought, "Whatever you do, don't hit it into that creek," is often followed by just that. We've all been there, and it certainly isn't play. So to return to golf as play, you have to watch your thoughts closely, something few, but Zen masters and their students, are trained to do. This is where the driving range can be a good training ground.

First, since there is no stress on the range, you'll need to create your own stress to get used to letting it go. Get mad at a bad shot. Go ahead: Slam your club down. Curse. Shake your head in disgust. After the hacked shot, take as many more balls as needed with that club until you've hit at least two good shots in a row. Three shots, if you're particularly pissed off. To get back to pure play, you'll need to get better at this game, and the range is the place for this. Nobody's watching. It's just you and your mind and your body and your sticks and a ball that sits like Buddha on the turf. Don't worry, Buddhists don't think Buddha is God. You can hit him as hard and as often as you want. No guilt. There will be no riots. He just leads the way to waking up and playing again. Alan Watts used to say the universe is having a ball with all its round objects and orbits. So have a ball with the Buddha balls on the range. We all have a lot of conditioning to overcome. Bad habits, the worst of which is negative self-talk, can creep into our playtime. So slam down those clubs, curse, kick the dirt, until you are beside yourself, laughing your ass off at how silly you look and how ridiculous you feel and how you must appear to others as you throw your golf tantrums like a toddler denied his toy.

Then, when the laughing subsides, return to golf with a half smile as the great Vietnamese Zen master Thich Nhat Hanh advises. With full awareness, take hold of the club, feeling the texture of the grip, the heft of the clubhead, the beauty of forged steel. Take a few swings and get in touch with your natural athleticism, with the shifting of your weight from back to forward foot, with the synchronization of your arms and your body. Return to your practice with a renewed sense of determination and hope on the journey to better, that journey of play that can literally heal your golfing soul.

HOLE 12
Seeing

THE BUDDHIST PRACTICE encourages the meditator to slow down and notice what's around and inside you. If you look closely and intently enough, the seer and the seen are indistinguishable. Golf is the perfect game to practice this as it takes place in beautiful surroundings, putting the golfer in touch with the earth and all its wonders. Individual golf courses, situated in the forest or by the sea can be awe-inspiring, beckoning you to count your blessings as you play this intriguing game.

Slowing Down and Looking Around

Dustin Johnson was remembering his meltdown on the final day of the 2010 U.S. Open at Pebble Beach and had an insight into what he should have done. Johnson took a three-shot lead into that final round, with destiny sitting there like a siren beckoning him toward the rocks. Right off, he made triple on the second, double on the third, and bogey on the fourth. By the time he walked off the fifth green, his three-shot lead imploded into a four shot deficit. Johnson shot 82 that day, relinquishing the laurels to a steadier Graeme McDowell. "Things kind of spiraled after the triple," he told the *San Francisco Chronicle*. "I

started moving fast, thinking fast, walking fast. I learned I really have to slow down with everything—my routine, my swing, my thought process, my walking. I've just got to take everything slower."

It's a great lesson for all of us. Ballooning to double or triple on any particular hole requires a regrouping, a pulling in on the reins, a breathing mindfully, a slowing down. This is not easy to do if you, like most of us, live a fast-paced life of running around doing errands, getting things done, and then falling exhausted into bed at the end of the day. Like golf, slowing down requires practice. In Buddhist meditation, which is referred to as "the practice" and the student as "the practitioner," the sine qua non of meditation is slowing down. It is 180 degrees from daily life. First, we sit and still the body. Without a still and quiet body, the thinking mind cannot slow down and observe closely as it needs to do at times. For most, that mind is constantly in motion during waking and sleeping states. Anything in constant motion eventually wears out. It needs rest. It needs silence. I remember living near a huge pine in the woods of New Hampshire. Now I live near 2,000-year-old redwoods in northern California. They live long, resilient lives. So we need to learn how to still the body as these trees do. In golf, that means a consistent pre-shot routine, a quiet, relaxed address position, and a mindful walk to the next shot.

What is a mindful walk? It is when we are aware of the distinctly human act of walking, of our feet touching the earth, of our arms swinging, of the breeze in our hair, of the sound of birds. This is not a constant, unbroken awareness, but it is one where we step back some in consciousness and see the big picture of our lives in that space of time. So we may be talking with our playing companions about what course they usually play or something about Tiger or Phil or Rory, but we also give thanks for eyes to see the mountains beyond the course, legs to walk eighteen holes, and hands to hold a club. When we reflect on our healthy body that allows us to be out enjoying playing this magnificent game, we slow down as a half-smile comes to our face. This is a mindful walk between shots. At a meditation retreat it might take you a half hour to walk the twenty-five yards from your room to the dining hall. That is mindful walking to the extreme, and it is a useful thing to do from time to time. On a golf course, that would get you into trouble with the foursome behind you, not to mention your own playing partners. So mindful golf walking is not super slow but is a broadening of your perspective, a widening of your awareness, and in doing so, your mind becomes more relaxed, more patient, more receptive, and quieter.

A relatively quiet mind allows us to gently sip and savor more moments, especially in our leisure hours—precious hours that give us respite from the often stressful work hours, and even the retiree hours when we have to devote increased attention to health issues, honey-do projects, family obligations, and the mundane assortment of never-ending errands.

Padraig Harrington, who is known for over-analysis and negative thinking around his golf game, dropped precipitously in world rankings since 2009. And this was after having won three majors. At the previously mentioned Open at Pebble he was in contention but hit an iron shot badly. "I hit it heavy because I was changing my mind every few seconds," he told the *San Francisco Chronicle*. "I probably changed my mind five or six times during that swing. When you're competitive, you make a decision and stick with it. When you're coming in a bit raw, you just don't get that commitment." The Irishman needed to slow down that runaway mind of his considerably. A lesson for all of us, he needed to gather up his game, pick a swing for the day, look around, and let it fly. He needed to swing his arms between shots, look at the sky, listen to birdsong, and slow the pace a bit, until he reached his ball. At that point, this notoriously slow player needed to size up the shot, make a club selection, and pull the trigger.

The slowing down I'm talking about then is between shots, and by doing so you won't need to get obsessive and fret over a shot like Woody Allen might over the thought of death. On the contrary, your overall play will speed up, making everyone around you happy. I think too it will lower your score as your body, especially your head, is stiller, more relaxed, more apt to rely on its natural athleticism. This will allow better contact with the clubface, wiser decisions around course management, and a rhythm unencumbered by worry and negativity. Then golf transforms into a dance—that ultimate art where no footsteps are left yet all footsteps are noted.

The Course and the Land

One of my favorite courses, Adobe Creek in Petaluma, went belly-up bankrupt a few years ago (it has since returned, bought by a courageous consortium), and news sources are corroborating this trend throughout the U.S. In 2013, for example, a remarkable 158 eighteen-hole courses closed, compared with fourteen that opened, up from 13.5 the year before. Adobe Creek is a Robert Trent Jones Jr. design that is thoughtfully laid out, and drains away rain like a bathtub. This consummately playable course lay fallow for several years, which was sad to see and deprived me of golf on a course where I once had a hole-in-one. Golf courses are forms of art, as buildings and gardens are forms of art. You can tell when care went into the design of a golf course. The course itself is a living thing, shaped by the designer's eye, hand, and spirit. You have to have a feel for the land, a feeling for its essence. The land can't be bullied, or grossly bulldozed. The land prescribes the course. The course is within the land as a sculpture is already inside the block of marble in the hands of a master.

A golf course is a combination of form and function, choreographed into art with a purpose. And that purpose is threefold: to entertain, to challenge, and to take the golfer to deeper levels of the game. The experience is visual. Elements like old mature trees, rustic bunkers, tranquil ponds, raw sea and sand, waterfalls, creeks, and a backdrop of hills and mountains are manna to not only the eyes but also to the soul. The course brings the other senses into play as well. The sounds of birds and breeze. The taste of salt air. The touch of earth under foot. The smell of pine and pitch and fresh air.

In my opinion, there is no place that epitomizes such interplay of elements as Pacific Dunes Golf Links in Bandon, Oregon. It is not just terrain to behold externally. The course was laid out by nature and nudged into form by course designer Tom Doak. He did this like a Zen roshi guides his student to the edge of rational consciousness then removes the last peg of platitude. No more bullshit. No more rationalization. No more intellectualization. What lies before you is pure, raw, and as rambunctious as a mustang. I swear Pacific Dunes moves under foot. And above ground it is almost ghostlike in the ubiquitous fog and wind and mist. The course doesn't hammer you like a heavyweight, nor does it slam you like a sumo: instead it lifts you like an angel, plays with you on silky clouds, then drops you like the rain you often encounter there.

You have to go inside yourself to play Pacific Dunes. You should do that for all courses you play, but PD subtlety and uniquely guides you in that direction. It's exhilarating and a bit unsettling to feel land guiding you in that way. We are used to gazing at the passive landscape, being affected by it, yes, but not directed by it. PD is anything but passive. Massive, jagged-edged bunkers, inheritors of ancient sheep taking refuge from the Scottish winds, stand guard with gapping mouths ready to swallow you and your ball. One required me to descend wooden steps into a sandy hell about as big and steep as a quarry. I couldn't see the green, the flag, or the sky. Smashing it out, I flew the ball over the green, losing it in the gorse. Round One, PD. Bunkers like that force you inside yourself. There are no reference points to hang your ego hat on. If you hold on to what you know, you won't be able to approach the shot with a sense of controlled abandon, a quality of letting go which golf requires. The bunkers at PD are another of its examples of the Zen Master manifest.

The lay of the land, too, most of it in view of the wild ocean, affects the psyche. It is like a wild cathedral, this land carved from the Oregon coast. It is spiritual in that it quiets the mind and brings out the best in a person even when that golfer is playing poorly. You won't remember the poor shots but you will remember the land and the course for the rest of your days. I know I will, as I will remember Zen Master Joshu Sasaki Roshi, who took me so deeply into my True Self.

But even your local muni can take you to places you never suspected you even wanted to go. It may not have the power of Pacific Dunes, but if you approach your round with awareness and consciousness, you allow the land to work its collective magic on you. Thousands have walked there before you in pursuit of fun and relaxation and camaraderie. Lions have mingled with lambs, peaceably, on such gentle battle fields. Yes, a golf course is also a kind of battlefield as a meditation hall is a battlefield. You are confronting aspects of yourself that trigger dissatisfaction, frustration, and downright anger. Golf brings it all up to the surface, which happens to be connected to a body walking on a golf course that reflects your level of concentration and consciousness. Carry that lousy putt on the last hole with you beyond the putt itself, and your next shot will probably find trouble. The master designer has figured in all the permutations and combinations of how the course will punish the perpetrator, namely the golfer who has fallen from the grace of the present moment into a deep, cavernous bunker of despair and ecstasy woven into a tapestry of self-discovery.

At the Home of Golf

To the outside world, the name St. Andrews stands for where golf was born. About 600 years ago, I imagine, since no one really knows, some shepherd picked up a stick of some sort and a ball of another sort, probably out of boredom, and started knocking it around, adding a hole in which to bat it into, and golf happened, discovering itself really. It was there all along, I surmise, perhaps from the Big Bang itself.

Of course that's just my perspective. I've been addicted to golf since I was fourteen, mesmerized by Arnold Palmer at that time, along with the rest of the country. Visiting St. Andrews has been an enduring dream, one that was running out of steam as age advanced. But some dreams do come true.

A couple of years ago, on a Sunday, Ruth and I strolled the Old Course, the oldest golf course in the world. It's open to the public to do so every Sunday, closed to golfing. I had hoped to play the course, but that dream would have to wait, as extra special dreams often do, given the Royal and Ancient Golf Association would be holding its spring meeting the entire following week. Later that day though I did play the Eden Course, one of nine connected with the town, in rain, sleet, and hail. I think that makes me an honorary Scottish golfer! The *Garden* of Eden it was, and the memory of that round and the town of St. Andrews will stay with me until my dying day.

Eden is a traditional links course, dating to 1914, the year World War I started. Links golf is much different than parkland golf as it has no trees and not much inland water, save for narrow, winding creeks the Scots call burns. What protects it involves wind, weather, huge undulating greens, tough gorse, heather, Scottish broom, tight fairway lies, and bunkers. They are tough SOBs, links land bunkers, deep and dangerous, requiring good course management and accuracy to avoid them. Put some troops up against those ramparts, and it's World War I all over again.

You've got to keep your wits about you and think your way around a links course. Course management. It's something amateurs know little of. We're too worried about technique and swing thoughts and making good contact with clubface at impact. Course management is somewhat more for pros. Links golf is more a ground game than an air attack, involving chip and runs and run ups where you play short of target and let it roll up to the cup.

Greens are hard and fast, and balls don't hold when flown at the pin. I went to the Golf Museum at St. Andrews and inspected many antique clubs—clubs designed with such a game in mind—clubs designed to meet the demands of links land conditions. Of course, my game is geared to lush fairways and greens that hold so I struggled some, much as I did at Bandon Dunes in Oregon. But once you get the hang of it, links golf is great fun and very challenging. There are a few hills to negotiate but mostly smaller mounds presenting challenging lies. Its greens and fringes are true, with the putter being the standard implement, even from considerably off the green's surface.

SEEING

Eden has a good practice facility, with mats, and if you pay extra, grass. So I got a half hour in, then started my round, solo, as no one else was playing that afternoon with storm clouds threatening. As I approached the first tee, sleet, hail, and wind started pelting and lasted the next four holes. I was layered in clothing like a cake, leaving me vulnerable to a course I knew nothing about. Eden slammed me hard. Bogeys and doubles. My swing was gone, encumbered by a bulky parka for protection against the elements. But golf being golf in Scotland, the weather began to clear, I found my swing again when I was able to peel off the layers. I started reading the greens much better. Pars followed, four in a row, and Eden and I began to get chummy.

Funny how a relationship can change with a golf course during a round. It involves more confidence in your swing, sure. One good swing, one great putt can do it. But the course begins to yield something of its defenses. The weather and the wind play into it. Luck too is a factor. Eden got friendlier, more accommodating. Eden offered some breaks. Maybe some compensation for my disappointment in not being able to play the Old Course. These courses at St. Andrews are all in communion with each other. Being relatively close to Findhorn, there is something strange going on here.

I only had time for twelve holes, but there was a time in history when that was what a standard golf course consisted of. The last six clicked though, even with rented clubs, and will stay with me for a lifetime. Some rounds are like that. I'll remember forever playing Pacific Dunes, America's greatest links course. I'll remember playing Bandon Dunes the next day, first time using a caddie, who helped me read greens like Evelyn Wood. I'll remember my three holes-in-one— one at Indian Valley in Novato, the other at General Washington outside Philadelphia with my brother Hank as witness, and the third at the fifth at Adobe Creek in Petaluma, California. I'll remember a 77 on our demanding muni Bennett Valley, and a 78 at Adobe Creek, with three birdies that day, the last one the result of the purest 6-iron I've ever hit, finishing just eight inches from the hole on the difficult

18th. I'll remember a round at La Quinta in Palm Desert on perhaps the best-maintained course I've ever played.

But for my greatest golfing memory, I return to the Eden Course at St. Andrews in the rain and wind and sleet, especially after I was able to shed a couple layers and get my swing going and sink a few putts and blast out of an impossible bunker to within three feet of the hole. Ah, 'twas a great thing to be golfing in Scotland. Aye, a great thing.

Links Golf at its Finest: Bandon, Oregon

There are basically two kinds of golf: links and parkland. Links courses are usually built on sand dunes next to the open sea. Parkland courses are built inland, among trees, and, these days, houses. Links golf originated in Scotland, where the game developed. Traditionally, it was a public land shaped fiercely by weather—wind, rain, sleet, fog—elements that act to defend and toughen up links land courses. Links golf is rugged golf. Walking is often required; power carts are often banned (you need a doctor's note to get permission to use one at St. Andrews). Among the best in the world is Pacific Dunes (PD) on the southern Oregon coast, as one of five courses in the complex that comprises Bandon Dunes Golf Resort. I've played them all—all gems in their own right. And power carts are banned here as well.

A number of golf magazines have identified Pacific Dunes as one of the world's greatest, and I heartily agree. Visually, it is as vivid and passionate and wild as a Winslow Homer painting. The Pacific Ocean, of course, is its ever-present namesake, wielding a wild brush of wind, water, fog, sun, rain, sight, and sound. The course was carved from sand dunes, native beach grasses, gorse, and wind-battered shore pines. Trees can't much stand tall and upright in these conditions. And sometimes, with wind and storm beating mightily, neither can a golfer.

The architect Tom Doak had his challenges, for to craft a golf course by the sea, you've got to do some bulldozing. But he worked his dozers gently like the arms of a praying mantis, pitching sand only when needed, letting the land itself lead a path to the routing. Doak's guiding principles were fairness and fun, although you'd better bring your "A" game to have a taste of both. Wind up in a PD bunker and you'd better bring a flask down with you.

Did I say that Pacific Dunes was voted the best of "100 courses you can play" by *Golf* magazine? That's the best as in one ahead of Pebble Beach, the so-called Mecca of American golf. I've played Pebble, and PD—without houses, carts, or slow play—is a better golfing experience. Pebble has history, yes, and it has beautiful ocean vistas. But Pacific Dunes has within it the very soul of golf.

I will also remember with equal fondness the three generations of the Rudawsky family from St. Louis I played with the first time.

Young Tommy, a high-schooler with a swing like R. McIlroy's who played from the tips; his dad, Basil, who seemed always to sport a smile despite where his shot ended up; and Basil's dad, Tom, whose knees may have complained that day but you wouldn't know it from his positive disposition. And none of us will forget Tom's reaching the Par 5 15th in two and two putting from sixty feet for a bird. They and their three caddies put me in the company of true golfers and true gentlemen.

That's one of the great things about Bandon: you meet some wonderful people from around the country. Like the second day at Old MacDonald. Except for the monstrous greens, the course didn't impress me that much. But Steve and Cindy from Bozeman, Montana, and their caddy Bucky did. Bandon golfers love the game, and this married couple was no exception, especially Cindy who was just two years into the game and would literally jump for joy when she struck a solid shot, which was often off the tee. She was experiencing a feeling I first felt at fourteen when I took up the game: that moment when the club makes solid contact with the clubface. It's why this game is so infectious. It's why we keep returning. Cindy broke 100 for the first time that day on a very tough golf course (Old Mac was rated number nine just behind Bandon Dunes in *Golf* magazine's list). We need people like Cindy and Steve to grow this game.

Day three, I played Bandon Preserve, a sweet, thirteen-hole Par 3 course, designed by Ben Crenshaw and Bill Coore, with a view of the ocean from every hole. My companions this time were Bob McVickers from Columbus, Ohio, and his son Ryan from San Francisco. These two are part of the reason I often prefer to go out as a single when I play golf. I get to meet wonderful people who I would never have had the chance to meet had I not ventured out alone. For golf is a friendly playing field, where people can meet via common interests and passion. When I started playing as a young teen, I was quite shy. Golf helped me crawl out of my shell and find the confidence I knew was within but needed the venue to bud and blossom. I still wasn't great with girls, but my Overbrook High School golf team, of which I was second man, won the Philadelphia city championship in '63.

Day four, I was back to Pacific Dunes, one of the three Audubon certified courses at the resort, this time with a caddie to help me read the daunting greens. Andrew was sixteen, and a caddie in training, in the running for a Chick Evans scholarship, which provides young caddies, who would not ordinarily have the means, an all-expense paid scholarship to the University of Oregon in Eugene. The Bandon Resort has the largest such caddie scholarship program in the United States. Good kid. And a great green reader.

Links golf is probably not for every American golfer, but it should be experienced at least a couple of times. Bandon, with its crown jewel of Pacific Dunes, is where I go to get my occasional fix of golf as it was originally conceptualized. Golf challenges our comfort zones. It puts us in positions at times where we'd rather not be, like behind trees and in water and inside a gorse bush. But we are golfers. We choose to be challenged. We have courage to take on the elements. Golf is the real reality show, without props or scripts or contrivances, and there's no better place for a golfer than the courses at Bandon Dunes to test his or her mettle.

HOLE 13
Challenge

G **OLF IS A** challenging game—arguably the toughest of them all. Why? There is too much time between shots to think of what you've done and what you are about to do, and of the resulting pressure around results. It is a game where success and failure are so intertwined, you'd better know how to handle both. As in life, those who succeed are tempered by failure, and how you relate to failure. Do you allow it to corrode your disposition, spoiling the rest of the round? Or do you feel its sting, learn from it, let it go, and move on?

Playing Badly and Staying with the Game

I know, when you play badly, it's tempting to want to quit this bloody game. You want to go home after a bad round, take the clubs out of the trunk, put them into the garage, cancel your subscription to the Golf Channel, and be done with this game now and forever. Hell, I've done that several times. Once for a year or two, I recall. But by then, the game was already in my blood. It lay there like a dormant, ancient seed buried in the glacial ice, ready to germinate at the first ray of sunshine after a great thaw. Eventually, it did sprout, that seed of golf, and I returned to the game that was now a part of my DNA.

But it leaves a scar, that leaving. It leaves a memory of isolation and loneliness being away from a game that teaches so much about life. I've been twice divorced, and it's kind of like that. You never fully forget those kinds of leavings. They temper all future relationships and leave you a little limp as you face the huge challenges ahead. After leaving long-term relationships, which golf is, you look for the courage to return, because once you've been burned that pain stays in the memory for a long, long time.

I did return, always conscious of golf's potential to produce fortune or misfortune, in the span of one round, yes, but also in the span of a lifetime. If you let this game get you down and you leave, it won't teach you a whit. But if it gets you down and you stay with it, you will eventually find a treasure chest of wisdom. For life, itself, will at times get you down, and your response to that will determine which direction you will travel. The great French existentialist writer Albert Camus once said the only real decision in life is whether to commit suicide or not. And if you decide not to, you'll need to take full responsibility in facing life head on. As I've written in a previous book, my first wife chose the suicide route and gave up the challenge of dealing with physical and emotional pain. It's a stretch to relate that horrid event to giving up golf, but it is relevant. All of us golfers have had the experience of no longer being willing to deal with the pain of playing bad golf. So we back off. We regroup. We put the clubs away for a while. That's fine. Sometimes we need to ease the pressure and relent and reflect and supplicate and let the golf gods have their way. There's a time for grinding, and there's a time for letting go and letting be.

Letting go, though, is tough for a golfer, or anyone, in this culture. We're hardwired to hold on tight and make it happen. Plow through it. Just do it. Don't quit. Hang in there. I was like that, but Buddhist practice helped me see it from a different perspective. I learned that all life is a matter of how we view it individually. That is, all of us see life and its moments from our own unique kaleidoscope of experience and genetic makeup. We are in relationship with every thought, every action, every drama, every decision that life requires. The key idea is relationship, and if we are going to learn anything about ourselves within those relationships, we need to not bail out too quickly.

I've counseled people who seriously contemplate, and, at times, have tried to end their lives. I listened to them and suggested other options. Sometimes I asked them to make a commitment to rehabilitation. But ultimately, it was their own inner view that reigned. How did they see their lives? With hope? With courage? With strength? With weakness? Did they have support? Did they use their supports? Like an addict in a twelve-step program, we have to take inventory of our life views, and decide if they are working for us. My ex-wife let go of life itself, robbing herself of the opportunity to grow and develop into a more conscious human being. For a fully conscious person is not someone who no longer feels pain or experiences suffering. It is someone who does feel pain and suffering, and decides to stand firm and face these challenges. Even if you decide to run after standing firm—after all, that may be the wisest choice—at least you acted out of sizing up your view of the situation. The conscious person knows himself and doesn't let fear or anger or any emotion bully him around. He assesses the situation, decides on options, and acts with the full faith and confidence in her own mind and heart. She is one who has left the nest, relying on herself to find her way on life's journeys. She takes responsibility for the obstacles encountered, and her reaction and relationship to them.

And this includes the journeys that golf takes us on—those thrilling journeys that require wisdom, discipline, patience, awareness, mindfulness, courage, abandon, joy, fearlessness, and faith in ourselves. Play is as much a part of life as work, love, and food, and golf is that Great Play that reminds us that disappointment is often the door that opens to reward and success. And even if those rewards and successes vanish in the next splash of a golf ball in a water hazard, we have a view that carries us through to the finish. With golf, there is always that element of hope that things will change for the better.

The Hardest Thing about this Game . . . and How to Take it On

Simply said, golf is a hard game because of expectations and what happens inside us when expectations are not fulfilled. Recently, I went out with the expectation of doing well, of maybe breaking 80, as I had done the previous August for the first time in many years. I had gone to the range and practice area the day before and the swing seemed sharp, the chipping was solid, and I was striking the sweet spot on the putter blade. My foursome wimped out on me, so I went out alone the next day, met some great guys at the course, and started my quest. It was about as perfect a day for golf as there could be. The first hole saw a so-so drive, but the next shot was a perfect 5 hybrid from the rough, to twelve feet above the hole. Missed the putt but an opening par was just what I needed to rev up my expectation engine. I'll spare you all the details, but I went three-over par for the next three holes, and a leak developed in my goal-for-the-day fuel tank. I was getting seriously demoralized, especially after chili-dipping a chip that led to a double on the fifth. Don't know what chili-dipping is? Believe me, it's not anything good. Five over. Damn. There goes the 70-something I had envisioned myself attaining. I could feel myself starting to press, and the pace quicken on my full swings. I could feel doubt enter my mind over subsequent chips and short putts. Now here's where the hardest thing about this game comes in.

Somehow, I managed to pull in the reins, and give myself a bit of a lecture. You know this game, said I to myself: fortunes can change quickly, and often for the best, if I only could recover from the last few holes. My mind was in failure mode. I had that hangdog look and the easy joking with my playing companions was replaced by silence: clinical silence. I can turn this thing around, I muttered to myself. I have the skills. My swing is solid. My putting has always been good. Just put the previous holes behind you and start over. Over the next three holes, I made three regulation pars. At the ninth, I made a great bunker shot to four feet, and a sand-save par, 41 front. And I am back in the old ballgame.

The point is I never stopped looking for small swing changes that could extricate me from the slippery slope of declining confidence. I was down but not out. In life, I've been there as well, as have most of us. You make adjustments. You try a different direction. You assess where you're at in that particular moment. You check your mood, realizing it can change like a shark does his direction. Nothing in life—no emotion, no circumstance, no attitude—stays the same. Change is a constant, more certain than taxes, and only a notch less certain than death. Knowing that is the key to escaping an increasingly poor round of golf in progress.

On the back nine, more leaks sprang but I kept plugging away. A regulation par on the 10th kept the par string going, and I'm thinking, "OK, maybe some possibilities here." But after a sweet, low, drawing 6-iron around a tree to the 11th green, I three-putted and the castles started burning again. Careless approach shots and poor chipping hammered me with bogeys and doubles in the next few holes. Again though, I gathered my forces, found something inside that was willing to turn and I came around with two late pars to finish with an 84, respectable for a winter's day in northern California.

I had salvaged a round that could have easily gone into the graveyard, and I did this with one part determination, one part golf sense, one part letting go of negative emotions, and a large dose of Zen. The Zen part had to do with literally dragging myself back to the present after lousy holes and poor shots catapulted me into remorse, anger, regret, lamentation, and utter frustration. The present offered me another chance. It offered salvation. It offered a clean slate where I could chalk a fresh version of my round. To paraphrase that somewhat hackneyed expression, "This next shot could be the first shot of the rest of the round."

That's why golf is a meditation unto itself. If you miss watching a breath in meditation, if your thoughts stray, if you fall asleep, there's no guilt involved, there are no confessions, there's no sin: you just become aware of where your mind and body are, bring them back to the present, see them for the changing states they are, and start over watching your next breath. It's not an easy practice, for the mind and body are so conditioned that once they tumble from the path of the present, they are lost and lame for a time, sometimes a lifetime. So the burning castles of golf . . . and life . . . are great opportunities to tackle adversity. They are great opportunities to shake yourself awake and come back to the truth of the moment, namely that freedom happens when you see that adversity is just the other side of the same coin of opportunity.

The bogeys and doubles will still come, but you'll be free of them in your mind faster, and open the door for more pars (or better) as the round continues. Then you will welcome the hardest thing about this game, and use it to stay sharper, more focused, and that much closer to whatever your golf goals may be.

Understanding and Using Pressure

We've all felt it. A tightening of the muscles around the neck. A lump in the throat. A rising of blood to the forehead. A quickening heartbeat. Sweaty palms. In golf, it's particularly troublesome, we are told. It's a game that requires precision timing and coordination. It requires being in the moment, dealing only with the matter at hand, namely wielding an unwieldy metal club, attempting to hit a small white dimpled ball to a target over 300 yards away. Any tightening, sweating, beating, or blood rising beyond the norm will truncate that process and dynamite any chance for success. We feel it elsewhere too, like at work when the supervisor comes by and asks to have a "word with you," or when a cop pulls us over, or when our spouse "needs to talk." Pressure greets us almost daily with its bared teeth and a scowl. An overdue phone bill. Noisy neighbors that need admonishing. Humans have always known it. We have much experience dealing with it, yet it's as difficult to handle now as it was in the caves of France thousands of years ago when some jerk was noisily carving a stone at 3 a.m.

CHALLENGE

In golf, no tournament is as pressure packed as a match play event. Every hole is as pressure packed as the last, and the last may well be your last before your flight home. How do these guys handle it? How do they maintain their level of concentration? How do they keep their swings from crumbling into bloody pieces? Matt Kucher was humming along during the 2012 Accenture Match Play tournament, making it to the finals until he ran into Hunter Mahan who started winning holes with pars, a sign that the loser of those holes was suffering from a tiny blockage in his mind. Pressure coming from within. The pressure of despair. Before the round, Kuchar told a commentator that he tries to play the course during match play. At least that's the plan. Nice idea, but when your opponent is shadowing every flaw in your game, it's time for some serious strategizing. Time to realize that in match play, the course is not playing you: your opponent is. Pressure comes not from the course but from the human being playing against you.

Even in a friendly weekend game, pressure comes from others watching you, along with you watching yourself. Expectations. You went to the range the day before and you were hitting it lights out. You started expecting a personal best round the next day. And just the opposite starts to happen. A few good shots result, but increasingly you start throwing shots away. Internal pressure builds like air in a filling balloon. Some shots produce embarrassment, *vis-à-vis* others in your group looking away in silence as you slam your club to the turf in dismay and disgust. Just the other day this happened to me. "Fifty years of playing this game," I muttered under my breath, "and I can still hit shots like that." I contemplated walking off the course. I came very close to breaking a club. So much for mindful golf, I thought. I soldiered on, trying to reconnoiter and regroup and somehow find my rhythm, like a jockey looking for that encouragement that might spark his losing steed.

Pressure in golf is situational. It can change as fast as that racehorse can come alive. As a meditator, I realize that if I can let go of the previous moment of disaster, then I can open the door to the next moment of potential glory. It's why golf is such a powerful spiritual practice. On the par 5 5th at Bennett Valley that day, I hit a beautiful drive, right down the middle, setting me up for a par or birdie. My expectations were high. Much praise issued from my boon companions. Confidence brimming from within as I strode down the broad fairway. Next a 4-wood to set me up for an easy wedge. A waggle, a swing, and I cold topped the shot. From victory to defeat in one swing. Pressure. And the rest of the hole I'm in catch-up mode. In golf, pressure is always there, waiting for the mind to let down its guard.

So pressure is a function of the mind. And the way to alleviate pressure is through the mind. That's the good news. The bad news is that if you alleviate pressure, you take away the incentive to improve your game. "Whuh? Whadat you say?" the crocs in the comic strip "Pearls Before Swine" might ask. Now, my Buddhist friends may not appreciate this but meditation will calm your mind and make you peaceful and content, but it won't necessarily get you what you want in life, including lower golf scores. Equanimity is one of the supposed goals of meditation. But with golf, and much of life, the goal is a combination of the West and the East: equanimity while achieving your goals. For many years I misunderstood the Buddhist approach, thinking that one had to sacrifice goals and achievement for equanimity. In relation to life, the understanding I've come to is that both are possible. Pressure, in fact, is the key. Buddhists, though, call it a sense of urgency.

These concepts involve a sense of time, namely time running out. In meditation, that sense of urgency derives from the body's inevitable march toward death. We know we only have a limited time to attain enlightenment—that state of being that transcends spiritual death. The practice of meditation has within it an element of pressure. Buddhist teachers always remind us there is no time to waste. Western teachers also remind us there is no time to waste in the living of our lives. They are always telling us to set goals higher and higher, to study, to work hard, and, when you fall, to "pick yourself up, dust yourself off, and start all over again," as an old song goes.

In golf, whether it's a single match, a club championship, or the Masters, the clock is always ticking, whether we are twenty-six like Rory McIlroy, forty like Lee Westwood, thirty-nine like Tiger Woods, or sixty-nine like myself, we are always running out of time to accomplish our goals. We feel pressure, and that pressure drives us forward, creating a sense of urgency that reminds us of why we practice, why we study, why we want to achieve, why we want to lower our scores or drive the ball twenty yards farther or chip and putt like champs. Pressure is not the bogeyman we make it out to be. It is the fifteenth club in our bag, fully legal, to help reach our golf goals and help us deal with the ever-present sense of urgency.

HOLE 14
Class Acts

IN GOLF, WE look to professionals as models of near perfection, men
and women who play a game amateurs can only dream of playing.
At one time, they were derided as lower class tradesmen who weren't
allowed in member clubhouses. But pros today are handsomely paid,
glorified, and held in high esteem. How they play the game, and how
they live their lives are on display for all to see. Sometimes they show
great courage and grit. Sometimes we see their grace. And sometimes
we see the pain of defeat on their faces. But either way, we are grateful
they have chosen to take on a life where failure is around every corner,
in full display of the TV cameras and reporters' questions. It's a life
most of us wouldn't dare take on, with our insecurities and lack of confidence. But watching them helps us realize the possibilities, inspiring
us to "hang in there" in the face of disaster and embarrassment.

Hail to the King: Arnold Palmer

John Hawkins, the bad-boy *Golf World* writer and Golf Channel commentator, said a while ago that he didn't want to live in the past,
commenting on Johnny Miller's remarks that there were more players who could close the deal on Sunday back in the day, namely his

day. Hawkins didn't want to look back at golf history ("I'm tired of living in the past," he barked), but golf is all about history. Present-day players perform with the past shadowing them, and those who ignore the past strip their game of perspective and inspiration. One of the greatest icons of golf history is still with us: the King, Arnold Palmer. When I was a kid there was a phenomenon known as Arnie's Army: the King's Army. Fans couldn't get enough of this guy who hit it a mile, not caring particularly where it went. He'd then dig it out of whatever dirt or rough he landed in and pull off shots only Hollywood could dream of. Arnie twisted his head, tugged at his pants, and flexed his artillery arms like Rocky Marciano going for the kill. In 1960, seven shots behind Mike Souchak at Cherry Hills and starting the final round of the U.S. Open, Arnie, with his Army at his heels, drove the green on the 346-yard first hole (with a persimmon driver and a balata ball!), one of the greatest shots in golf history. He went on to birdie that hole, chip in for birdie on the second, drive it into the trees on the third, but in typical Palmer fashion find an opening, keeping it low, and making birdie, scoring 30 on the front nine, and going on to win by two. Who was second? Amateur Jack Nicklaus. Third? Ben Hogan, going for his record fifth Open. Souchak faded to fourth, and Arnold became a legend, throwing his visor in the air and dancing on that last green in triumph.

Remarkably, that was the only U.S. Open Palmer ever won, despite several close playoff losses. But the King won seven majors in all, a great feat. He also lifted golf from a genteel game of well-off folk, to the image of a working-class hero from western Pennsylvania's coal country, with guns for arms, hatless, tanned, robust, confident, gracious, and always willing to stop and sign an autograph, with a smile, for a kid or a grandma. It was a healthy, hardy time for America, a heady time, with JFK in the White House, Cassius Clay in the Olympic ring, and Arnold on the golf course.

I took up golf because of Arnie, as did many kids in those days. My sports were baseball, football, and basketball, but Arnold Palmer was compelling enough to get me to try a sport my family didn't know much about. I got hooked quickly, and stayed with it as I aged, as did Mr. Palmer. In fact, there were times I got very discouraged with my game and considered quitting. But when I discovered that Palmer was frustrated too with his game as he aged, I thought, well, if Arnie isn't quitting the game neither will I. Once again, he was an inspiration for me, this time to hang in there, persevere, try a new theory, and hit it hard while keeping at least some control over it. Palmer showed me how I needed to modify my swing as my body changed. Shorter backswing, stay in balance, head steady, use the new technology, and stay in shape. He also showed all of us that golf isn't just a good score: it's time with friends; it's keeping a good disposition no matter what; it's giving back to a society where we have such tremendous opportunity; it's having integrity, compassion, and composure; it's acknowledging and honoring people from presidents to plumbers. Arnold Palmer was and is a mensch, a Yiddish word for a decent, responsible person with admirable characteristics: a true human being.

I was watching the Arnold Palmer Invitational a couple years ago, and there he was, holding court. The players respect him enormously, and what he did for golf. Tiger put a gold, monied edge around the profession, making many ho-hum pros millionaires, but Arnold set a platinum standard. Solid, respected, exciting, even swashbuckling and courageous. I was fortunate to see Arnold play in his heyday, alongside a young Jack Nicklaus at the Whitemarsh Open in Philadelphia in the early 1960s. It was unforgettable, with Palmer tossing his cigarette down and hitting laser, low-trajectory drives out of sight, and Nicklaus (an unpopular Nicklaus because the Army didn't like him beating their hero so much) hitting these high, soaring shots that seemed launched into space. Palmer lamented to Jack about the cameras clicking away around them during their swings, while Nicklaus nodded in agreement. For a fifteen-year-old kid, only Jack Kennedy's campaign swing through Philly affected me more. I was a very shy kid, going through some rough teenage years, but seeing the King charging down the fairway, hitching at his belt, smiling at the crowd, gave me a hero to model myself after. I was part of Arnie's Army, something important, bigger than myself.

Kids need that, perhaps more today than ever. Kids need heroes that don't fall, for if heroes fall in their personal lives, kids lose faith in the integrity of those heroes. So when faced with tough decisions—whether to steal or not, whether to use drugs or not, whether to stay in school or not, whether to join a gang or not—they need to have a hero's compass to help them navigate their way through. Arnold Palmer was such a compass for me.

And for the young, strong pros of today, they shouldn't just be looking at an octogenarian, wrinkled legend when they pass by his viewing stand on the 18th at his beloved Bay Hills. They should be looking at and remembering the young, strapping bomber who greened a 346-yard par 4 at what's been called "the best damn Open ever," and who went on to close the deal after being seven shots behind. Still want to disregard the closers of the past, John Hawkins?

Phil

He has been with us longer than Tiger now. He has played in the wake of Tiger, sometimes awash in that wake. As Tiger has made several major swing changes, Phil has essentially stuck with the same swing. It's familiar to us, his fans. He approaches the ball like a gladiator, pulls the trigger, whips back his flail just past parallel, and unleashes a drive that no one, no where, knows exactly where it will land. He looks apprehensively to the right or the left, as do all golfers in heaven. The very earth tilts farther in the looking. Quakes and volcanoes trigger. Rivers flood. Fish leap. Mountains slide. Golfers spill their beer. Phil tips his cap. Earth breathes a sigh. He's in the fairway.

Phil Mickelson is a good guy. People pull for him. People want him to win, especially lately. Phil is running out of time, and it shows. He has some kind of arthritic condition, the name of which sounds much worse than arthritis itself. Phil has experienced a perfect storm of maladies. His wife Amy had cancer, as has Amy's mom. One of

Phil's daughters had a seizure and spent the night in a hospital. This shouldn't have happened to one as blessed as Phil, but Phil takes life, and golf, as it comes, with a strong dose of courage and guts and perseverance.

Phil has won five majors, to date. That puts him in the higher echelons of golf history. Like Sam Snead, he has, to date, never won the U.S. Open, the one he truly covets. He knows, we all know, his majors total should be double that, and not just because of Tiger. Phil takes chances. Phil the Thrill, they call him. A train wreck waiting to happen. Here it comes! Sometimes it works out: miracle of miracles. April 13, 2010. A six-iron from the pine straw between a gap in the Georgia pines on the 13th at Augusta, against his caddie's advice, over Rae's Creek, to a sloping green. Again, that swing. So much courage in that swing. So much recklessness. So much piss and vinegar. Brazenness and bravado. Or was it, "What the hell! Gimme the goddamn six-iron, (his caddie) Bones! I'm goin' for it." He nailed it, landing it like a hummingbird four feet below the cup, going on to win the Masters. That's why we love Phil. He makes us all proud to be golfers. Phil doesn't bunt. Phil doesn't play a ground game. Phil jump-shoots from three-point range. A lot.

Since his amazing win at the British Open in 2013, Phil has been struggling some, but he keeps showing up. He keeps trying and he keeps tipping his cap and he keeps smiling that smile that we don't often see in professional golf. Phil's smile is a smile that embraces the universe. It says, "I like you folks. I'm here not just for myself but also for all of you. I love golf, not only for what it's done for my family and me, but for what it teaches people about life. I'm a happy man, even when unhappy things happen to me."

Will Phil win another major? A U.S. Open? It really doesn't matter, but yes, I think he will. Five puts him in the realm of Raymond Floyd, minus the Open. Phil is not a freak of nature, as is Tiger Woods. He has more of an everyman quality, with real feelings, with honest answers, with humble mannerisms. Phil will play to the fullest every time he enters a tournament. He will give himself fully to the crowd who cheers for him. He will devote himself to his family. He will talk earnestly to the press. He will honor the game in the tradition of Bob Jones. He will treat his caddie well. Jim "Bones" MacKay is virtually a family member. He will know when it's time to quit competitive golf. He will continue to help the community through his foundation.

Phil Mickelson is a golfers' golfer. He's a mentor to younger players at the Ryder Cup and Presidents Cup. He shows how one should play as a pro. Swing from your heart. Connect with your fans. Keep trying. Believe in yourself. Honor your fellow competitors. Honor your spouse.

I love it when the old Phil appears. Like the other day at the Humana Challenge, when he took only twenty-four putts on his way to a 66, hunched behind the ball, the closest thing to Jack Nicklaus as Jack Nicklaus. He's got his old putter back too, as standard as Crenshaw's, Faxon's, and Boss of the Moss Loren Roberts. His putting though has often left him the past couple years, 2014, in particular, when he failed to win a tournament. Not so his magical chipping touch, but his putting, yes. It's sad to see. It must be the arthritis. The nerve endings must be blunted somehow, like railroad signals shut down and gone awry. Nerve endings that always got the putting trains to run on time now in a jumbled mess, missing three and four footers, leaving Phil shaking his head and slumping his shoulders and the fans moaning. It's not quite like seeing Mohammed Ali now, but it's not far off. But still, those days appear when the confidence returns, bursting through the haze covering the cup, and twenty-four putts and a 66 shine through.

Go see Phil if you get a chance. He's an inspiration to follow during a round. He'll teach you how to be responsive to what's around you between shots, and be absolutely focused during the shot. He'll teach you how to walk and swing your arms, how to smile and acknowledge a fist bump from your fellow players. He'll show you something about playing golf from a higher position of consciousness and bravery and honor.

CLASS ACTS

Ken Venturi

Whenever I think of Ken Venturi, the late Hall of Fame golfer, I remember that determined, iconic figure shuffling down the last fairway of the 1964 U.S. Open, dehydrated and barely able to stay on his feet, let alone swing a golf club, gritty as an Olympic decathlon champion only needing to cross the finish line of the 1,500 meter race to win the gold medal. I was seventeen at the time, watching the spectacle on our family's black and white TV, literally praying Mr. Venturi wouldn't collapse in front of the world. The temperature in Washington, D.C. that June day was over one hundred degrees, and players had to endure a thirty-six-hole final, the last such year for that requirement. It was a test of skill and conditioning on the highest levels.

His gait wobbly, Venturi removed his Hogan cap as he approached the 18th green, waving to a cheering crowd. What a moment in golf history! Whenever I need inspiration and motivation to persevere with this impossible game, I think of that moment and smile at Ken Venturi's will and resolve to finish in the face of extreme adversity. After all, a doctor had told him after the first eighteen, that to continue on could be fatal. "That would be better than the way I've been living," he replied, as we all learned later. Venturi laced up his shoes and returned to the withering heat and potentially lethal consequences.

After his playing days were over this former stutterer faced another challenge—becoming a distinguished and revered golf commentator for some thirty-five years. But it is the warrior who faced down death and won the Open who I will most remember and admire.

Thank you, Ken Venturi, for all you gave to golf, the game you loved.

Ernie, Autism, and his Legacy

Ernie Els is a man of high integrity. The Big Easy is also a fabulous golfer. But he will be just as remembered for bringing to the public's attention the plight of autism. His young son Ben, is autistic, and Ernie and his wife Lisl bravely chose to reveal this and form a foundation, educating the public about this tragic and debilitating illness. As a counselor with over thirty years in the field, I've worked with people with autism and related Asperger's syndrome, and can tell you it adversely affects every aspect of life, both the individual's and their family's. There are different levels of autism, ranging from complete separation from others, such as rocking and obsessing on the movement of their fingers, to a social disorder, of varying degrees, where the person is of above normal intelligence but has difficulty communicating and making friends and relationships. I've worked with autistic kids who can only rock in a chair all day, absorbed totally with themselves, and others who've gone on to college and work. The entire illness is now known as the Autism Spectrum, with a wide range of functionality.

There's been much misunderstanding, fear, and prejudice around autism over the years, as there has with most mental disorders. With people like Ernie Els stepping forward and sharing his son's and his family's struggles, he has done a tremendous service in clearing the air and helping raise money to find a cure or better treatment approaches. But mostly, Els has taken a cloak of ignorance off this illness and has let some light into the lives of children and adults who have been pushed into the darkened rooms of shame and sadness.

There is a place in our society for everyone. Everyone has value. When Ernie carries his son around after a tournament, he honors every parent with an autistic child and says to these children everywhere, "We love and honor you. We see you. We will be there for you. And we will forever remind society that you are the sons and daughters of us all."

To contribute, go online at http://www.ernieels.com; or send a check to:
Els For Autism
11770 US Highway 1, Suite 102
North Palm Beach, Florida 33408
www.elsforautism.com

Jack

There are some golfers in history who have earned the right to be known primarily by their first name, and Jack Nicklaus is one of them. His major accomplishment is just that: he holds the record for number of professional majors won—eighteen. He also won two U.S. Amateur titles. He was a slow, methodical player who hit towering drives and irons into the center of greens. These led to pars and birdies, which led to Jack winning many tournaments, worldwide, both on the PGA Tour and the Champions Tour.

Unlike his main rival, Arnold Palmer, Jack was not well liked when he first turned pro in 1961. That's because he consistently beat the King of Arnie's Army. But Jack was a class act who bore down and concentrated on the matter at hand: beating Old Man Par, as Bobby Jones, another class act, referred to competitive golf. Through persistence and determination, Jack eventually won the hearts of golf fans, and became much admired and praised as the years went by, especially after Arnold faded as a competitor in the early 1970s.

Beyond golf, Jack and his wife Barbara went on to establish a foundation that has given millions to help thousands of hospitalized children in Ohio. Today, Jack also designs golf courses worldwide. The Golden Bear is and will ever be one of golf's truly class acts.

HOLE 15
Fall from Grace

***

BETWEEN 1996 AND 2008, Tiger Woods dominated professional golf like no other player in history, with the possible exception of Jack Nicklaus. He had it all: one of the greatest golfers in history; fourteen majors won; married to a beautiful wife, father of two lovely children; founder of an educational foundation that helps kids discover their potentials; friends with other sport legends; rich beyond all belief; held in high esteem wherever he went; and one of the most widely recognized figures in the world. But around Thanksgiving 2009, all that changed for Tiger Woods and the entire golf world. In golf, as in life, fortune can change to misfortune as quickly as "the swish of a horse's tail," as the Buddha said.

Tiger's Fall from Grace: Meditation and Golf

At a Tiger Woods news conference in February 2010, in the wake of his sex scandal, his most significant revelation was that his troubles started when he stopped meditating, when he stopped practicing the Buddhist religion, which he shared with his mother. That's when he lost his moral compass. Being a Buddhist, Tiger is involved with more than a religion. In fact, Buddhism, at its core, is more a spiritual practice than a set of beliefs that comprise most religions. As the late philosopher and Zen-popularizer Alan Watts once said, "Buddhism never uttered its final doctrine." Essentially, through trial and error, the practitioner finds out what is the truth for him or herself. It's a path that requires taking total responsibility. You can't retreat to God or a set of truths to guide you: you are the captain of your own ship. It's why monotheistic religions often don't buy into Buddhism: there a basic belief human beings need help, and that help comes from a higher power. These other religions involve prayer and meditation just like Buddhism, but with the Buddhist system of practice, the higher power is essentially called your True Self, or that part of you which is always in the present and not subject to birth or death. It's a part of you that is always available to you, if you can get in touch with it. When you meditate according to Buddhist instructions, you simply stay with your own body and mind and breath in the present moment. When Tiger stopped meditating, as he admitted, it was tantamount to his stopping practicing his golf swing: he got out of practice and forgot some of the fundamentals involved in being a true human being. When that happens you can begin to hurt yourself and hurt those around you who you love.

In life, and in golf, the present moment is the only real refuge we have. It's where it all happens, for better or for worse. If our thoughts stray elsewhere during a golf swing, we're at high risk for dubbing the shot. In daily life, if we are not attending to the matter at hand, accidents can happen, the wrong word can pop out of our mouth, anxiety can replace serenity. Buddhists call meditation "the Practice," simply because it is practice for staying in the present moment. In Tiger's case, he could no longer see the consequences of his hedonistic actions because he lost control of his ability to see and understand himself—the deepest pit a human being can fall into. Removed from the sanctuary of the present, he was floating in an abyss of self-deception and lies—floating alone without the support of his inner circle. Buddhists call that inner circle the *sangha*, or community of fellow meditators. The problem with Tiger's sangha is that it consisted of only one person, really—his mother, who was also his teacher. When he lost touch with her, which it seems he did, he lost his only sangha member and meditation teacher. Since the Buddhist does not rely on a God to walk this life with, he needs the sangha to help remind him of what is important about what the Buddha called "the Middle Way."

Tiger's friends, since they were not practicing Buddhists, were not part of his spiritual sangha. Nor, it goes without saying, were his mistresses. So he was virtually isolated—from his friends, his mother, his children, his wife. All he had really was golf. And, as he admitted at that news conference, golf was no longer any fun. A Buddhist, like a Christian, a Jew, or a Moslem needs a supportive group around him or her to help keep a proper perspective on life.

Tiger won a good many tournaments as a result of that meditation practice of his. He was quite skilled at staying in the present, following up bad shots, and whole rounds, with spectacular ones, and staying absolutely focused on applying the pressure and intimidating opponents. Honing your swing may not be enough. You may need to add meditation to your daily routine. Now I can just see half of you returning to your beer and putting down this book. Meditation? Who me, my church pew on Sunday is the first tee box. Nah, I'll skip the spiritual stuff.

But I'm here to tell you meditation is very powerful, both when you employ it when Tiger did, and when you don't use it as Tiger did also. It's not difficult to begin meditating. It is difficult to treat it seriously and stay with it once you start. If you're willing to consider it, your golf game will benefit and become an extension of your meditation practice. This does not involve a change in religion, by the way. You can meditate and keep your current religion. In fact it may enhance your connection with it and bring you closer to your inner self and whatever higher power you believe in. And that may help keep your mind, and your head, still, which may well improve your golf game.

What Golfers can Learn from Tiger

With the sex scandal of Tiger Woods well behind us, the average golfer can learn much from one of the greatest golfers in the history of the game.

- First, as Yogi Berra famously intoned, "It ain't over 'til it's over." Pundits, including myself, continually predict the end of the Tiger Woods era. But the only person who can count you out and convince you that you're finished is you. Tiger has responded to all his crises and physical dilemmas with hard work, perseverance, and determination. He has never been ready to lie down, roll over, and call it quits. With five wins and Player of the Year honors in 2013, the man showed true grit in grinding it out and digging himself out of a deep hole. Back surgery in 2014 was his newest challenge, but, again, his golf career "ain't over 'til it's over."

- In any given round of golf, like life itself, fortunes can change as quickly as the swish of a horse's tail, as the Buddha put it. It all depends on how the mind relates to what just happened. A few years ago, Kenny Perry was leading the Senior PGA until he lost that lead on day four with a double bogey on the par 3 13th. "I hit a good shot," Perry said. "I could have stood there and told you, when that ball was in the air, I was thinking that thing is in the middle of the green. I couldn't believe it flew the green. So either I got a bad yardage or something . . . I don't know. It's one of those deals. I can't explain it . . . . That kind of shocked me a little bit. I couldn't believe it went that far, for one thing. And then I was in jail the whole time. So to make double on a hole that you think you can make birdie on, that hurt." The quote gives you a peek inside Kenny Perry's head, and shows you why he never won a major on the PGA tour. Would Tiger Woods have been shocked by such a mis-play? No. He would have put it behind him immediately after watching it sail the green. You can do the same with your mis-hits.

- In golf, there is always room for improvement. And, as the body ages, you must have the flexibility to modify and refine your swing. Tiger Woods has been criticized over the years for continually working on his swing despite success. He's overhauled his swing entirely several times. Why not just leave it alone? If it it ain't broke, don't fix it, as we say in the States. But Woods knows the golf swing is not a static entity. It can change in subtle ways. The body looks for comfort, and the golf swing is not a natural motion. As water always seeks the lowest point of flow, gravity exerts its constant influence on the human body. The golfer, especially the professional who earns his or her living from the sport, must be aware of how these changes are manifesting in the swing. A grooved swing changes over time. And a changed swing causes trouble if the golfer is not aware of where those changes have occurred. Tiger is constantly monitoring his swing, working on conditioning the body, and making changes where necessary, under the trained eye of a coach. And so can you.

- Tiger Woods has a tremendous will to win. He plays with passion. He plays with commitment. He plays with determination. He is a serious athlete. He plays with a strong sense of golf history. And so can you.

- Woods loves to practice, and does more of it than perhaps anyone who has ever played the game, including Ben Hogan, the next best at practicing. He can do that because he's in shape. When he heals from specific injuries, which we all encounter from time to time, his body can handle the punishment of practice. You, too, can get in shape. It takes determination, inspiration, and perspiration. I joined a gym in 2011, and have benefited greatly. I've increased my practice time as a result, and have lowered my handicap from 12 to 8.4.

- Woods is mentally tough, and moves on after bad shots or bad rounds. He seems not as affected by the ups and downs of tournament golf as his contemporaries are. True, he seems way too guarded in the pressroom after these events. But there is still something to learn, namely to not let the game rattle you. Move on after wayward shots or big numbers.

- Tiger devours everything golf. It's his life, after all. You too will want to be as involved in the game as he is. It's your avocation, which is just as important as one's livelihood. On your deathbed, will you give more thought to the job you had or the times you broke 80? I hope to have a club in my hands at the time, getting that grip right.

- Put your money to good purposes. Tiger's foundation, which he formed with his late father, Earl, has helped thousands of kids through this sometimes arduous journey called life. On a smaller scale, there's the First Tee, which needs volunteers, helping the USGA out at a tournament, or contributing to a Boy's or Girl's Club. Whether it is money or time, there's a need you can fill.

On the other hand, as we've seen in the past, Tiger Woods is no model citizen. But we can take the best of Tiger and learn from him, and leave the rest behind in the dustbin of indiscretion and human frailties.

HOLE 16
The Majors

WINNING EVEN ONE professional major tournament, of the four in golf, signals a player had a stretch of play where everything came together: physical, emotional, mental, and spiritual. Majors are played on tough golf courses, made even tougher than usual by those in charge. And because they're so difficult to win and sought out by so many of the game's greats, the pressure is enormous. They are tests not only of a player's skills but of his or her character in the face of stakes that will change a life forever.

Majors winners literally go down in history in the most positive of ways, much different than other events on tour, where fans' memory of a win might last one or two years, if that. If a player has a major to his credit, the press, the fans, and the entire golf world remembers and mentions it at every opportunity for the rest of the golfer's life.

The U.S. Open Honored

The United States Open is arguably the greatest tournament in golf. It is open to all comers, for one thing. If you qualify, you're in. True, that is a daunting proposition. Even well-ranked touring pros don't make it, so if you do qualify, it's a real accomplishment. Open courses

are tough, set up to punish any wayward shots. Since it's played in June, the temperatures are often hot and baked. U.S. Open greens are as slick as pool tables but with ridges and breaks and false fronts. Three-putts can send the Open competitor into mental misery faster than a meter maid writing a ticket. And the whole world, seemingly, is watching.

When I was a kid I'd fantasize about playing in the U.S. Open. Those were heady days of hope when Palmer and Nicklaus were slugging it out, Kennedy was in the White House, and I was second man on my high school golf team, a clinically shy kid who could chip and putt my way to pars. Obviously I didn't realize my Open dreams, but I'd watch the Open each year and be there vicariously.

1960: Palmer charging from seven behind to take the title.

1962: Nicklaus with those booming drives and deft putting touch to best Palmer on his own turf, Oakmont.

1964: Ken Venturi walking a kind of Bataan death march up the 18th at a scorching Congressional with the title close at hand, no one assured he wouldn't pass out like a marathon runner turning into the Olympic stadium.

1965: Gary Player blew a three-shot lead with three to play, but came back to beat Kel Nagle in an eighteen-hole playoff, winning his only U.S. Open, and completing a career Grand Slam.

1971: Lee Trevino, the former U.S. Marine who bested the Golden Bear in a playoff and would go on to be Jack's main rival in the 1970s, amassing six majors.

1973: Johnny Miller shot one of the greatest rounds of golf in the history of the game, a 63, coming from six shots behind competitors like Palmer, Player, Nicklaus, and Trevino to win his only U.S. Open.

1982: Tom Watson came to the 17th at Pebble, the Pacific Ocean at his back, tied with Jack, who was looking to win his record fifth Open. In a shot ESPN called the greatest in golf history, Tom holed an extremely difficult short-sided downhill chip to pass Jack and win by two for his only U.S. Open victory. Recently, when Jack was asked what was the most memorable shot of his career, it wasn't any of his own: it was Watson's amazing chip.

And who will ever forget Tiger Woods, hobbled in pain, beating journeyman Rocco Mediate in 2008 at Torrey Pines, nailing a twelve-footer to tie, then tie in an intense playoff, finally putting away his third Open on the 91st hole in sudden death? Some of the greatest drama in sport history. The Open brings it up and out.

How does this particular tournament do this? It's the venue. The golf courses are set up in such a fashion as to be intimidating and in some years, diabolical. Either the pin placements or the rough or the length or the narrowness of the fairways or the speed of the greens are manipulated to produce the toughest conditions on the planet, conditions that will shake the confidence of the greatest of players. Try to imagine fourteen on the Stimpmeter. The other day I played on greens that measured ten and I three-putted five times and four-putted once. I had my worst score in about twenty years, vindicated only by two birdies that restored my faith in the redemptive possibilities of golf.

The players at the Open, under the microscope of the media and the glare of millions, have to be fine-tuned in mind and body. Their concentration must be such that they are in a kind of bubble where all sounds and sights extraneous to the shot before them cannot penetrate the delicate membrane of the bubble; where all thoughts of fame or glory or fortune likewise cannot enter the bubble surrounding the mind; where not even a single wish or desire can crack the sacred space of the present moment. For if one stray thought of negativity enters the bubble and bursts it, a Pandora's Box of embarrassment, fear, insecurity, shame, anger, self-defeat, disgrace—all of these, summed up by Phil Mickelson at the 72nd hole at Winged Foot in 2006 when he shot double bogey, losing his best chance at winning the Open ever, sat off the green with his head in his hands, muttering, "I am such an idiot."

The Masters: Then and Now

More than any other golf tournament in the world, the Masters carries a mystique that elevates golf to the gods. In 2014, Gary Player, Jack Nicklaus, and Arnold Palmer, three of the greatest who ever played the game, hit ceremonial balls off the first tee to start the tournament. Can you name another tournament that starts like that? All past Masters winners gather for a dinner the night before the start to feast on a meal sponsored by last year's winner. Can you name another tournament that does that? The Masters was conceived and developed by Bobby Jones, winner of the Grand Slam in 1930, and perhaps the greatest golfer ever, all equipment considered. Can you name another tournament with those bona fides and ancestry? While we still debate whether to call The Open Championship the British Open, only one word is needed to identify the Masters, worldwide. And a win (or a loss) at the Masters can define a career.

Take Fred Couples, when, in 1992, we all held our collective breath as his tee ball somehow stopped on the steep embankment in front of the par 3 12th green. One more turn and it would have tumbled into Rae's Creek, his Masters hopes dashed as he battled the formidable Raymond Floyd for the title. In 1996, we remember the loser much more than the winner. Greg Norman took a 6-shot lead into the final round, only to lose by five to Nick Faldo. Faldo shot 67 to Norman's 78, after a 40 on the final nine holes. Viewers were stunned, remembering 1987 when Larry Mize pulled off another Norman conquest. Mize, Norman, and Ballesteros tied after regular play, heading to a playoff. Seve was out after the first hole, leaving Norman and Mize to battle it out. Mize came up short at the par 4 green, leaving a difficult pitch to get down in two. Norman was safely on, a good distance away for birdie, but a sure par. Greg said later he didn't think Mize could get down in two. He was right: Larry Mize got down in one as he holed the pitch for birdie to win the Masters and once again sink Norman's ship.

Greg Norman lost yet another Masters in 1986 to a charging Jack Nicklaus, in perhaps the most memorable Masters in history. Jack was forty-six at the time, hadn't won a major in six years, nor had he won a tournament in two. Most considered his career at an end. But he came into the '86 Masters feeling and playing well, and had his son Jackie on the bag. A third round 69 put him into the mix, but he opened the final round five shots off the pace. No one paid much attention to the greatest golfer of all time, until the Golden Bear went birdie-birdie-birdie on holes 9, 10, and 11. He followed with a birdie at 13, and hit the green in two on the par-5 15th. Things got hot and very interesting when Jack rolled in a twelve-foot eagle putt to get within two strokes of the lead. Crowd noise became deafening as Nicklaus almost holed out on the par-3 16th, dropping another birdie putt. He then birdied again on the 17th, and parred the 18th to score the back nine in thirty strokes, for a final round 65. Then the waiting began to see if his 9-under round would hold up to the likes of Seve Ballesteros, Tom Kite, and, you guessed it, Greg Norman. As the golf gods decreed, Seve found water and drowned, Kite missed three straight birdie putts, and Norman, then ranked number one in the world, made four straight birdies to catch Nicklaus at 9-under. He came to the 18th needing a birdie to win and a par to tie. He pushed his approach to the 18th green well right, chipped up, and missed the par putt to drop out of the tie. Jack Nicklaus attained even further golf glory with his 18th and final major. Sadly, Greg Norman will not be eating at the Masters dinner for winners ever.

In 2011, Tiger Woods, who won in 1997 by an historic twelve shots, staged a comeback after his scandal and a corresponding lapse in his almost magical game. He hadn't won a major since 2008, but here he was just a few shots off the lead coming into the final round, trying for his fourth Masters win. Before the Masters, he won at Arnold's tournament, carving up that course like a surgeon. He had all the shots in the bag Tiger is known for, except perhaps his super ability to read greens. Woods, I believe, was the greatest green reader in history in his prime. But after the scandal, his divorce, and all his personal preoccupations, that skill had seemingly diminished. And in this Masters, perhaps in a portent of years to come, young Rory McIlroy from Northern Ireland led the tournament by four shots as the final round began. He held that lead coming into the back nine on Sunday, but duck-hooked his drive on the 10th, shocking the golf world, and himself, by making triple bogey. The internal earthquake continued with a four-putt double bogey on the 12th, fading to a final round 80 and well off the lead, in fifteenth place. Tiger Woods, who was seven shots back to start the final round, shot 31 on the front nine including an eagle at 8. He eventually tied for the lead, but a three-putt bogey on 12 and a missed five-foot eagle putt on 15 doomed his chance at a fifth Masters title. Woods has never come from behind in the final round to win any of his fourteen major championships.

Adam Scott stormed up the leader board and after a birdie at 16 he held a two-shot lead. Jason Day, another Aussie, made a thirty-five-foot birdie putt on 17 and another birdie on 18 to post –12, a share of the clubhouse lead with Scott. However the day belonged to South African Charl Schwartzel, who chipped in for birdie at 1, holed out for eagle on 3, and birdied the final four holes to win by two shots; his 66 was the low round of the day.

Who will win the Masters in the next few years? Rory McIlroy has to be placed at the top of the pack. Winning two majors in 2014, Rory is a phenom. Imagine a swan playing golf and call him Rory. This young man plays with grace and passion. He is fearless. He is fresh. He is friendly. If he can sink enough four-footers for pars, watch out for McIlroy. Tiger, though wounded after his back surgery, can still never be counted out. He's a dangerous player who loves Augusta National and knows every nuance and strategy to succeed there.

Stealth Golf at the British Open

Stealth golf on a weekend at a major tournament. The guy sitting on the lead in the 2012 British Open, the 141st, and oldest of all the majors, also known as The Open Championship, was Adam Scott, a great Australian golfer who had never won a major, had the most pressure on him. That was obvious. What was not obvious was how Scott played the last nine holes on Saturday. That performance tells a subtle tale. He hit many of his birdie putts short, which showed he was beginning to feel that pressure. It's a sign of any golfer feeling pressure but particularly touring pros who are in contention to win. The body, dictated by the mind, is protecting a lead and so his nerve endings in his fingers get a bit cautious around not hitting a putt too long, giving him knee-knockers coming back for par. And too many four- and five-foot par putts coming back will unnerve most human beings. In golf, a four-stroke lead can easily notch into nothing, spoke by spoke into the black hole of anonymity.

In the 2012 British Open, the stealth golfers were Tiger Woods and Graeme McDowell, peering out like panthers in the dark jungle. Scott could see these predators and knew they were there, waiting for him to make a false move, waiting for an opportunity to strike and wound their prey. And make no mistake, golf may appear to be a genteel game, but at the highest levels, it is *The Hunger Games*. Pros can tell interviewers, like Tiger Woods did after the third round, that he will just concentrate on his game plan and play his own game, but you knew he'd be watching Scott carefully for signs of stress and fatigue and failure. And McDowell, too, who took down Tiger a few years before at a tournament Tiger sponsors, would be watching Scott or whoever the leader was with the eyes of a panther.

A champion stealth golfer, particularly at the British Open where fortunes can change in a heartbeat, watches the field while keeping total control of his own game. He does not allow himself to slip down the leader board, always shooting for par or better, especially on the easier holes. He knows he will make the occasional bomb on the greens of the harder holes, but they are reluctant gifts from the golf gods, like the holed bunker shot Woods made on the 18th green on Saturday. The stealth golfer plays more a waiting game, an opportunist's game, a stalker's game, observing weakness in his opponent, keeping his emotions in check, breathing, calculating, focusing, pacing himself, then pouncing when the opportunity presents itself.

Tiger did not move as much on Moving Day, as the third day of any tournament is called, as he had in the past, missing birdie putts he used to routinely make. Scott showed signs of pressure and fatigue on the greens with that broomstick of an anchored putter. Zach Johnson, my original pick that year, shot the best round of the day on Saturday, and could be there if Scott folded and threw in his cards. Brandt Snedeker, who made a surprising comeback late on Saturday after a miserable round, seemed too erratic a player to maintain the patience needed for a panther. And then there was Graeme McDowell, a stealth panther if I ever saw one, who had been biding his time too long after his glorious win at the U.S. Open a couple years before. This was a stealth panther ready to win again on a grand stage. But it would be a tough and bloody fight with that other predator, who is trying to regain his position as leader of the pack, Tiger Woods.

The British Open, like most majors, requires consistency, increasing course knowledge throughout the four days, avoiding big numbers, and the patience to wait it out and let others around you get careless and go the wrong way out of contention. Because when you start dropping strokes in major tournament golf, the velocity of that loss of momentum increases like an avalanche. One of the greatest stealth golfers in history was right before our eyes in this 2012 Open Championship, namely Tiger Woods. He made a science of pars and birdies as he thinks his way around a golf course. Bogeys are anathema to him, considering them as arch an enemy as Sherlock Holmes saw Professor Moriarty. The guy mutters vile curse words to bogeys as he walks to the next hole, vowing to eradicate them from his scorecard like grease stains. For the past couple years before, due to his golf and personal life engine falling off track, he lost his stealth powers, but the signs were there that the old Tiger was back. As are all courses in the Open rota, the venue at Royal Lytham & St. Annes Golf Club was spiked with lethal bunkers, deadly and gnarly gorse, and nasty weather, so far playing possum that year, but ready to pounce on the unwary.

In a prime example of how stealth golf can unfold at the British, Scott was the leader after 54 holes at –11, with Ernie Els six strokes back, tied for fifth. After a birdie at the 14th hole, Scott was one over par for the round, but incredibly bogeyed the final four holes for a 75 and dropped to second. Els, two groups ahead of Scott on the course, birdied the 18th hole with a clutch twelve-foot putt for a score of 68 and the clubhouse lead at 273 (–7).

Entering the final round, Graeme McDowell and Snedeker were tied for second at 203 (–7), four strokes behind Scott. McDowell shot a 75 (+5) and Snedeker a 74 to knock them out of contention; Woods had a triple bogey at the sixth hole and carded a 73 to tie for third with Snedeker.

The "Stealth" Champion Golfer of the Year 2012 was Ernie Els whose -7 total took the title. It was his second British Open win, and, his fourth major.

The PGA Championship: Glory's Last Shot

The following account was a preview of the 2012 PGA Championship, played at Kiawha Island's Ocean Course in South Carolina, published in my blog, The Mindful Golfer, on August 8, 2012.

The pinnacle of golf lies in the majors. That's where the glory is. Nick Faldo will be long remembered after Colin Montgomerie fades into obscurity. Freddie Couples will also be remembered for his one win at the Masters in '92. And even unknown Steve Jones will go down in history for his U.S. Open win in 1996, while Luke Donald will be but an asterisk if he fails to win a major in his career as a pro, as John Cook is today. This will be a tough one, a rugged, demanding course that Ernie Els predicted will produce an over-par score to win it, calling it a "very difficult course." *Golf Digest* scored it "the hardest course in America." It's an ocean links-type course, at Kiawah Island in South Carolina, that unlike a true links layout, is best played in the air, not on the ground. Adding to that, they've had a lot of rain, making the course soft and lush. It was designed by Pete Dye, one of the best golf course designers on earth, known for his almost quirky, thinking-golfer layouts. Ron Kroichick of the *San Francisco Chronicle* called this course "devilish," and the moniker "Dyeabolical" has been used to describe some of his designs. Stray from the fairway and you enter a hellish rough with long sea grasses, and sandy areas that spectators can walk through. None of these areas are considered actual bunkers so players can ground their clubs, but under such unpredictable conditions how the ball emerges is a big question mark. PGA pros don't like question marks.

As for who will win, remember that sixteen different players have won the last sixteen majors. That doesn't bode well for repeat winners like Tiger Woods, Ernie Els, and Angel Cabrera. But among players with one major notch on their belts—like Rory McIlroy, Keegan Bradley, and Webb Simpson, young guys who know how to win—the course sets up well. It's long, about 77 million yards, with some wide landing areas, and soft, elevated greens, which demand good putting and chipping. Being on the ocean, wind is a major factor, along with rain, humidity, and as Rory pointed out, bugs, which swarm and bite. I moved to California because of biting bugs in New England, so I know of what he speaks. Bugs have caused mass migrations in the history of mankind. I have no doubt South Carolina has seen similar migrations out of the state.

Tiger Woods is favored, but he has not put together four solid rounds in a major for four years now. I do not think Woods will win. His drives will drift in the winds, producing big misses, and landing him in trouble. He will contend, as he usually does, but I don't think he'll corral his fifteenth major, in his obsessive march to best Jack's record. Ricky Fowler has short circuited as of late. He has too many hinges in his swing to be a consistent factor. Sergio Garcia desperately wants to play himself onto the Ryder Cup team, but desperate is beginning to define Sergio's career. Luke Donald is just not long enough to challenge the monster length of this course. And Lee Westwood, too, is beginning to have a desperate quality about his demeanor in majors. I predict Rory McIlroy, the young phenom from Northern Ireland will win. He has the swing; he knows the grass the greens are made of since it's the same as is used on his home practice course in Florida; he finished high in the Bridgestone Invitational last week, surging to the top ten; and he knows how to think his way around a golf course. Rory is ready to clear his mind of his famous girlfriend, and win again.

But who knows? When you figure that Rich Beem, Shaun Micheel, and Wayne Grady have won this tournament, and Arnold Palmer never won it, anybody on tour, given its depth, could have a great week and walk away with the Wanamaker Cup. At this level, the steadiest mind, which seems particularly to be at a premium this year, with guys wilting at the finish, will win.

*

So who won? Well, I was right: Rory McIlroy, and I consequently won a large water ice from brother Hank in Philadelphia (to be collected at some later defined date when I am on the East Coast and temperatures are well above 80 degrees).

Rory shot a bogey-free 66 in the final round to win his second major title, at the time, by eight strokes over runner-up David Lynn. The victory margin was a record for the PGA, surpassing the seven-stroke win in 1980 by Jack Nicklaus. The PGA has been held annually since 1916.

The Ryder Cup: Seve and the Value of Inspiration

I don't necessarily believe in reincarnation, but keeping alive the spirit and memory of the dead is a near-universal tradition that I do believe in. Such was the case with the European team at the 2012 Ryder Cup at Medinah in Chicago (the Ryder Cup is not officially a major, but it's just as important in its own right). Seve Ballesteros, the great, late icon of European golf, was with this team, in spirit, as they faced almost certain defeat, down 10-6, coming into the final day of singles matches, which U.S. teams almost always win. With Jose Maria Olazabal at the helm as captain, a great player whom fellow Spaniard Seve mentored during his career, the Europeans wore an image of Seve on their sleeves, as they grinded and gutted and putted their way to the greatest comeback in Ryder Cup history. It was a most noble way to honor the patron saint of European golf—this charismatic, passionate, almost swashbuckling, golfer who won five majors, ninety-one tournaments worldwide, played on eight winning Ryder Cup teams, captained another winning team, and is in the World Golf Hall of Fame. Seve was most noted for his courage, for his ability to take on any golf shot and find a way to pull it off, which he did most of the time. Such is what the Europeans certainly had in mind at Medinah when they steamrolled the Americans on the final day of competition.

Inspiration is a powerful arrow in the quiver of a golfer, even a weekend amateur. It can come from different sources, depending on one's personal history. It could come from a relative who gave you your first set of clubs or took you to the range as a kid. My mother knew nothing of golf but she drove me to the course every morning during summer vacations when I was a teen, and picked me up at night after my friends and I couldn't see the ball on the greens anymore. Would I have been so passionate about golf for all these years had she not done so? I don't think so. My father gave me his old set of Bobby Jones blades, its shafts painted to look like hickory. Would I have sliced a 5-iron on the grounds of my old elementary school, broken a window, and run like hell with one of my buddies, laughing all the way home, and never mentioning another word of it? Until . . . now, come to think of it! Oscar Langman, the driving range teacher in Fairmount Park in Philly, taught me the fundamentals in ten two-dollar lessons that turned into about a hundred free lessons every time I showed up, which was often. Would the game have gotten into my blood, as it did, if Oscar hadn't been so kind and understanding? Arnold Palmer drove the green on the first hole of the last round of the 1960 U.S. Open, and he went on to overcome a seven-shot deficit to win his only U.S. Open. Would golf have occupied my every waking hour during some emotionally rough teen years as I watched Palmer thrash his way out of trouble like Braveheart? No. Thanks, Mr. Palmer. And, today, at sixty-nine, my core getting stronger and my drives going longer from dragging myself to the gym after work everyday, I look at a poster at the facility of an older buff guy standing there with two dumbbells in his hands over the caption, "Getting old is not for sissies." I couldn't continually drag myself to this gym after work each day if not for that poster.

Inspiration gets human beings to go beyond what they think they can do, what their judging mind tells them they can't do, and do more. We see it in the news, on the sports pages, and in our own lives. I come out of work at five o'clock, crawl to my car like a sloth, trundle to the gym, and come alive when I see that old fit guy on the wall (along with a photo of Marilyn Monroe working out!). Inspiration and imagination perhaps convinced the first humans to leave Africa. How else would they have found the courage to venture into the unknown? Inspiration must have been with Ken Venturi, perhaps it was his mentor Byron Nelson, when he trudged through heatstroke to win the 1964 U.S. Open at Congressional. And something must have inspired the New York Mets in 1969, perhaps the Scarlet Letter of perpetual cellar dwellers, when they overcame an eighteen-game deficit to best the Chicago Cubs in the regular season, and then dusted the Baltimore Orioles in the World Series to become the first expansion team to win the Series, going from the "lowly" Mets to the "miracle" Mets.

At Medinah, the Europeans came in as underdogs, and promptly got behind in their specialties—foursome and four-ball matches. Putting usually defines the Ryder Cup and the Americans were making everything while the Europeans couldn't find the cup. The United States finished Day one with a 5-3 lead, snatching the momentum from the Europeans. Keep in mind the team of Tiger Woods and Steve Stricker was 0-2 by the end of this day. But Captain Davis Love III was smiling. Day two four-balls and foursomes again went the Americans' way, again with Stricker and Woods failing to win a point, and Woods benched for the first time in his Ryder Cup career. MVP Ian Poulter kept the Euros in the match by contributing to a crucial point at the end of the day, scoring five consecutive birdies, preventing an American 12-4 rout. The score after Day two was bad enough for the Euros: 10-6. It was not insurmountable but only the 1999 U.S. team, under the captaincy of Ben Crenshaw, ever came back to win from such a deficit. The pundits were nailing up the coffin of a European defeat, but they didn't figure on the Seve Effect. Luke Donald defeated Bubba Watson in the first match of the day and that was huge. His teammates saw the possibilities, especially after hearing Captain Olazabal inspire them with a talk that was essentially right out of Napoleon Hill, who wrote, "Anything the mind can believe, the mind can achieve." After Luke's win over Masters champ Watson, the Euros started believing. They won their next four matches, leading 11-10 at one point. Now they didn't just believe, they were achieving.

This is when the inspiration of Seve was most powerful. When Ballesteros smelled victory in his prime, there was no stopping him. And the same was true of the Europeans the rest of that Sunday. You sensed, and the eyes of Poulter foretold the results, that they couldn't be contained. It was *their* Cup, fought for boldly for the sake of their hero, personified perhaps in the body of their captain. The Ryder Cup of 2012 is now known as the Miracle at Medinah.

Inspiration. Find yours.

HOLE 17
Why Play?

GOLF ELICITS STRONG emotions. Some ridicule the game as being elitist. Some say it's baffling with its esoteric rules. Others, who have tried it, develop an aversion to a game that is extremely difficult and complicated, involving too much failure and scant success. My own father, with an ego the size of New York City, gave me his clubs, and never hit another shot. But for those who become captivated by the game, those moments of success, which are certainly elusive, but are extremely satisfying and emotionally powerful, are legal opiates that draw the player in most pleasurable ways.

Why We Play this Game

I was playing with what might have been the worst golfer in the world the other day at the muni I frequent, Bennett Valley in Santa Rosa. A very nice fellow, Fred turned to me and asked, "Why do people keep returning to play this impossible game?" Fred might have had the worst swing ever, but he asked good questions. I myself have quit the game about five or six times out of total frustration but returned every time after varying hiatuses. Now, in my older age, I'm here to stay. So I have some direct experience with Fred's question.

My initial answer was that golf is a good example of a theory of behavioral psychology, of which, having been a psych major, I studied way back in college. It's called operant conditioning, and more specifically, intermittent reinforcement, the same principle that makes slot machines so exasperating yet so appealing. Simply, you play because of the expected rewards, even though the rewards might be few and far between. And the rewards, in golf and at the slots, are so satisfying that, like the addict, the player is willing to endure the agony to experience them. And all golfers, even Fred, have experienced those rewards. I watched Fred, retired though he was, dance a jig on the tee—yes, literally—after a particularly solid shot. And so powerful was the effect of that shot, that even after hitting just about every tree on the course with his next dozen shots, Fred retained in his mind's eye that one shot that propelled him into golf glory. He wants that feeling again and, despite all the self-flagellation, he will keep coming back until he gets it. And like the slot machine, you occasionally get a jackpot. In golf, it would be like Fred making a par, or even a birdie, or who knows, one day he'll break the bank and shoot a hole in one. It's happened, even to the worst of golfers on the worst of shots. (My brother Hank witnessed me get a hole-in-one once on a half-sliced 9-iron outside of Philadelphia a number of years ago.)

So why do we play this impossible game? After our boss points out our flaws, or our clients complain about our lack of attention, or our spouses complain about something we neglected, or our kids give us no respect, or our friends never call us, or a cop pulls us over for a minor infraction, we love reveling in that one good shot, that "Hey, great shot, Fred!" that high-five after sinking a thirty-foot putt, that great up and down from a bunker, that first time breaking 100 or 90, or, Hallelujah—there are angels in heaven—80. We come back because of a dream that is based in some reality. Golf throws us occasional crumbs, but those crumbs are so satisfying that they seem like sirloin steaks, smothered in onions. Golf feeds us—mind, body, and spirit—and there are few things in life that feed us like that. All it requires of us is to show up, endure the pain and suffering, accept what is, and smile broadly when the good stuff happens—kind of like life itself.

Hands, Head, and Heart

Two things connect you to the club: the hands and the head. One thing connects the hands and the head: the heart. To play this game you need feel, which comes from the hands; focus, which comes from the head; and passion, which comes from the heart. Take away any one, and most likely you're not enjoying the game. Like a bad marriage, you're just going through the motions. It's probably a game you should give up and take the clubs to Goodwill, or play once a year so you can still say you play but have a great excuse for why you play so badly or only whack balls at the range so you can use the game for therapy.

The hands are your only connection to the club. Take hold of a club, any club. Feel the grip, its texture, its lines. Notice its girth, how it tapers, how it telegraphs its subtle messages. Manipulate the club by holding it firmly and turning it all which ways. Whichever way your hands go, the clubhead goes. Go ahead, test it out. I'll bet the clubhead follows the hands every time. So what does that prove, you ask? What have I learned here that I didn't already know? Just that when you pick up a club to hit your next shot, consider the influence of the hands. Snead said hold the club as you would a small bird. But when you reach the impact zone, that bird may be a hawk. And you don't want to hold a hawk lightly when it's trying to fly away.

After the hands, the head comes into play with about a zillion things on its mind. The head has things on its mind? You bet. Just listen. Do I have the right club in my hands? How far to the target? What is the target? Which way does the wind blow? Can I clear that lake? I can give myself a better lie, right? Winter rules? OK, spring rules. You get the idea. Whatever the mind can believe, the mind can achieve. Only in golf, it more often works in reverse. The head has a way of questioning, of doubting, of weighing options. It has a way of holding on to the hot coals of the last bad shot, the last miserably read putt, the last wedge in the water. The head never seems to be settled, nor does it seem ever satisfied, nor is it willing to give up control to . . . the heart.

The golfer's heart comes at you with a big handshake and a Hi, How'ya doin? It plays this game with abandon and a grin and a hit it and find it and hit it again approach. It's helpful, this heart. It'll look for your ball, show you where to hit it, and where the collection areas and false fronts are. This golfer's heart wants you to do well. It's a generous heart. It was the heart of a Southern California man I played with the other day while on vacation in Palm Desert—a man who cheered us on and encouraged the other middle-aged men and women in our foursome, who helped read putts on greens he knew well, who filled in my divots with sand and seed, and who pointed out the trouble to avoid (if only I'd paid more attention!). He was a true gentle, friendly, and helpful man, who Buddhists would say received instant good karma by finishing the round on a tough Nick Faldo-designed course with two birdies, a par, and a bird on the toughest finishing hole in perhaps all of California for a 79 for this 13-handicapper.

Of course the golfer who most comes to mind when considering the epitome of hands, head, and heart is the legend who, sadly, died in 2011, age fifty-four, of a brain tumor: Severiano Ballesteros, better known as Seve. This man did for European golf what Arnold Palmer did for American golf. His hands were such that, in his prime, no shot was impossible. This amazing shotmaker could feel what was needed for any situation confronting him. "I have watched him play 1-irons out of greenside bunkers when just fooling around," Jack Nicklaus was quoted by the Associated Press. "He could do anything with a golf club and a golf ball." His course managing head was like radar sizing up any number of factors in about a second and transmitting that information to some situation room in his brain, which sent the final impulses to act to his hands. But all that was just mechanics, and Seve was more an artist than a mechanic. It was Seve's heart that added that touch of greatness that defined this man, and inspired an entire golfing world. Hands, head, and heart: Seve had the whole package.

Our goal as golfers is to piece that package together. That is the definition of success. The score is a by-product of our ability to weave together those elements in such a way as to create a beautiful cloth on the embroidered side and a minimum of loose threads on the underside. But near the end of life, the score will fade—witness Seve, Arnold, Jack, Bobby, Babe—and what remains is the mark of the man or woman.

The Last Round of Your Life

There will come a time when you will play the last round of golf of your life. It's near impossible to tell when that will be, so to take some control of this eventuality, I'd suggest treating every round you play as if it could be the last round you'll ever play. This insight came to me recently after playing one of the best rounds I'd ever played. I've had lower scores, but I'd never struck the ball as solidly, nor had I ever hit so many greens in regulation, nor had I ever chipped and pitched so crisply, nor had I ever stroked my putts so smoothly with correct line and distance so consistently. I played this round with two boon companions whom I had never met before, but were generous with their acknowledgements of my performance as it was happening. I ended the round quite satisfied and looking forward to the next opportunity to repeat this show of proficiency, and confirm that I'd risen to the next level of my golfing ability.

Well, that night after greeting my wife with the news of the day and receiving her congratulations, having a smooth eighteen-year-old Scotch, and easing my aging muscles and bones from a day of winter air and dampness with a bubble bath before dinner, I prepared for bed, as usual, by removing my pants and. . . . Now that's where this story takes a life-affecting twist, which eventually led to the writing of this piece. For in the process of removing my pants to slip into my pajamas, I tripped on the cuff of the pants and took a wild fall, smashing against a nearby chair in the bedroom. My wife, aghast, witnessed the entire episode, as I lay there winded, shocked, and stunned that this mindful hiker/golfer/human being had done something so unmindful in the process of so mundane and routine an activity.

But that's the nature of accidents, isn't it? We've done something a thousand times without incident, treating it with so much absolute matter-of-factness, that we drop our mindfulness for just a second and wham! we're flat on our backs, trying to assess the extent of our injuries. Can we hop back up, no harm done? Or, as in my case, lie there for a time, in semi-shock, knowing I'd done some serious damage as my ribcage hit the (fortunately upholstered) chair with what seemed like jackhammer force. At least I hadn't hit my head, I thought at first. As a mental health counselor who sometimes helps those with ABI (acquired brain injury), I thanked God and all the angels for that. It's one of the toughest disabilities of them all to deal with. I didn't hit my spine either so I knew that wasn't injured, another very tough disability. It felt like a bad bruise, and a bit later thought I'd fractured a rib. A couple days later, I had it X-rayed and was reassured the ribs were intact.

But two weeks later, as I write, I am still in pain and unable to swing a club. On a positive note, I've been able to practice chipping and putting since the fall, and seem to be sharpening that crucial aspect of my game. The bruise is healing, albeit slowly, as I apply ice, homeopathic cream, and take anti-inflammatory meds. I long to get back to playing and see if I could repeat the magic of that last round before the fall, but I'm being a good patient and holding my proverbial horses. But as most writers will do, I think about things: What if I were injured more seriously and I could no longer play golf? What would life feel like then? What would I do with my time? And, though I'd have the sweet memory of that last round, how would I deal with the realization that I would never be able to test whether I could repeat it? They were rather horrid thoughts, I must say. And, despite all my Buddhist training, frankly, I was freaked out by those thoughts.

WHY PLAY?

Yes, I learned that I needed to up my mindfulness levels, but still, accidents do happen. We can be driving perfectly well, and some alcohol-infused driver can rear-end us on the freeway. Or we can slip in the bathtub and crack something that might take years to heal. Or a boulder can dislodge as we are hiking just beneath it and . . . .You get the idea.

So given these possible worst-case scenarios, what can we do, despite our best intentions, to stay safe? For golfers, we can play that next round of golf as it were our last. We can focus on being absolutely present with each shot. We can leave troublesome thoughts behind us after we ready ourselves and our equipment, and head off to the clubhouse and the first tee. And when we reach that first tee, we can take a moment to look around, appreciate the sky, the trees, the grass, the breeze, the chill morning air, the beautiful hole in front of us, the fact that we are healthy enough to play that day, and give a moment of thanks. Yes, it's a prayer, of sorts, elevating this game of golf a couple of notches on the ladder of consciousness. It could well be our last round. After all, I was once hit on the back just below the shoulder by a screaming ball through the trees. A foot higher and I might not be here to write these words.

So I've been granted a reprieve this time. My deep bruise will heal, I'm sure, in time. Luckily, it's winter and it's wet and it's cold and there's mud on the ball with almost every shot, a good opportunity to chill out and practice the short game. The angels have been relatively kind, sparing me from serious injury, whispering in my ear the same message Don Juan, the powerful Nagual of Carlos Castaneda, continually whispered to him: Live life as if you have death, itself, hovering over your shoulder. That will certainly grab your attention, which is exactly what we golfers need to stay riveted to the task, and the fun, at hand.

HOLE 18

Home

—————

WE OFTEN PLAY golf with others. We play by ourselves too—and that's fine—but there's something about the joy of camaraderie that we like. The joy of spending time with kindred souls—laughing, commiserating, imbibing, bragging—remembering what we learned. To reflect back on a shot, which was particularly memorable, to chat about a professional tournament we just saw, or the exploits of a certain player we admire: this is also why we play this game. We want to feel connected. And after playing nine or eighteen holes, we've peeled off a few ego layers, perhaps, and have gotten to know someone a bit more. Lifelong friendships have started this way, with golf as the impetus.

But even if that's the one and only time you play with a particular person—and, in fact, that's what often happens when you connect with total strangers on the first tee—there is great value and pleasure in meeting new people on a peaceful and friendly playing field.

Camaraderie: Golf as a Contact Sport

One of the great attractions of the game of golf is contact with other people. And I mean direct contact, not just social media where a computer is the necessary means to connect you with others. Computers and social media have their value, but with golf you can go to a playing field, meet total strangers, and spend the next five hours together. Or you can gather there with your golf buddies, do some trash talking, compete, bet, check in on life happenings, compare golf equipment you just bought, talk Tiger news, make predictions about the pro tour, share insights about your game, give out tips, enjoy the sunshine, deal with the wind—all face to face, back to back, and belly to belly. Computers are silent beasts, but at a golf course, except for the actual shot, you make noise. You laugh, you yell, you beat your chest, you encourage a good shot, you lament a bad one. You emote. You exclaim. You put your head in your hands and moan when you miss a four-foot putt. You say "yes" and pump your fist when you make a 40-footer. Not another sport on Earth approaches golf for its ability to promote camaraderie in real, direct, personal ways. Feeling lonely and isolated? Go to a golf course, tell the pro shop you'd like to play with someone, and they'll connect you after a short wait.

A few Thanksgivings ago, I even got a tee time for Pebble Beach, one of the greatest courses in the world, which advertises a year wait, just a day before venturing out myself, joining a very agreeable threesome, one of whom knew this tough course well and could guide the rest of us as to the best lines and positions.

Some say interest in golf is waning, and that is true. But it will never completely die out. Why? Because it counters the anomie of our discordant society. It's a friendly game, marked by handshakes at the beginning and end of a round, by courtesy for the other players in your group and on the course. There is little discrimination on a golf course. Unlike a pickup basketball game where blacks usually play with other blacks and whites with whites, I've never seen golfers turn people of other races or genders or ages away when a single or two-some approaches the first tee and asks, "Can I join you folks?" All are accepted. All give their first names. Plumbers, teachers, judges, neo-Nazis, cops, therapists, lawyers, senators, prostitutes, priests, rabbis, and ex-cons are equal in the eyes of the greatest game on earth. Unless you ask, no one knows what you do for a living, whether you're a militant jihadist, or you're dishonorably discharged, or you're planning to blow up the clubhouse, or if you just robbed a bank and now have a million bucks in your golf bag. Nope. Like the Preamble to the Declaration of Independence says, We hold these truths to be self-evident, that all people are created equal, that they are endowed with certain inalienable rights, that among these are life, liberty and the pursuit of birdies. Or something like that. Regardless of handicap or horoscope, you pays your green fees and you gets to play. All I ask is that you don't walk on my putting line.

I started playing golf when I was fourteen, a pimply faced kid, full of fears and complexes and guilt. I was good at sports and school but essentially was a social misfit. Clinically shy, my first date was a blind one for my senior prom. I was depressed and anxious, like Charlie Brown, on my way to a lonely life ahead. Golf changed all that. Like the First Tee does today, golf taught me values that began to connect me to others. It was a solo sport, yes, giving me a socially acceptable space to experience my aloneness, but it was one that required me to be conscious of others. I joined my high school golf team, which got me out of myself and into a team mentality and awareness. I was happy when playing golf with my teammates, made friends, got out of my teenage angst, and even felt gratitude for my mother's support in driving me to the course on summer mornings and picking me up at night after a day of delights playing a game I loved with my friends. Golf (and other sports) saved me from my dysfunctional self, gave me a sense of pride and accomplishment, raising my battered teenaged self image, and helped me let go, at least at times, of worry, unhappiness, and despair. On the golf course, I could play and swing and feel the sweetness of the sweet spot and the ultimate pride of a 75, followed by a junior trophy and a 1963 high school City Championship Team letter.

The 1960s continued to be a tough time for me (and the rest of the country), amidst a social revolution, college, Kennedy's assassination, the Vietnam War and the draft, and my continuing malaise, but I always found some time to relieve the pressure by loading my persimmon woods and my blade irons into the car (now I was driving), heading out to Cobbs Creek in West Philly, and playing a round. I'd match up with whoever was at the first tee, and transport myself into another world where peace reigned, and people held the flagstick for you, and you could bomb a drive on occasion, and get up and down for a par, or sink a twenty-footer for birdie.

As life became even more complicated in my twenties and thirties, I golfed less and less, and that was a great loss. I didn't realize how much I needed this game for healing and perspective and connection. My inspiration, Arnold Palmer, faded, and no one else had quite the scintillating ability to inspire, including Jack who played a much more conservative, plodding, though brilliant, game. Palmer was a risk-taker, a shot maker with those arm-guns a-blazing. His flame fizzled, as age whittled away the sinews and nerves that made him great.

It wasn't until the eighties that I came back to golf, trying to reconstruct a game that had atrophied and devolved into a 20-handicap. I don't know what inspired me, except that I saw the possibility of resurrecting the game as a kind of fun way to meditate. By that time, I'd done quite a bit of work on myself through therapy and Buddhist practice, trusted myself more, and was more self-motivated and confident. I also recalled the memory of how it was in my high school days, when I helped lead my team to the city championship—that sweet, heady memory of laughing and playing with my teammates until the light was fading in the summertime, before my mother arrived, with me coaxing them, saying, "Come on, guys, let's go play the back five."

As for Golf, Above All, Have Fun

You hear it often when pro golfers are asked about their hopes for a tournament: I just want to go out there and have fun, they often say. Isn't that what playing golf is all about? We can often forget that and get very serious about the game. We slam clubs to the ground. We curse. We grumble. We threaten to drop this game and never return. Bowling or badminton would be better. It's a difficult game, sure, but it affords us many opportunities for success. Every golfer, at every level, experiences at least a few shots during a round that are fun, satisfying, and successful. Those shots give us hope that we can do this, that we have the potential to stick an approach shot near the hole, that we can chip it close to get up and down, that we can sink a thirty-footer for par, that we can smack a drive 210 yards straight down the middle, that we can break 100, or 90, or even 80. Golf is a source of much frustration and disappointment, absolutely, but it can also lead us through the gates of Shangri-La.

Golf is a game of honor, as well, a game of gentle men and women, where a Sergio Garcia can feel a sense of obligation to his opponent Rickie Fowler because he took too long working out a free drop on the previous hole, thinking that might have affected Rickie's concentration. On the next hole at the Match Play Championship a couple years ago, Rickie was in danger of losing the hole, but Sergio generously gave him a halve out of courtesy and generosity, odd though it seemed to some commentators. You don't often see that in other sports. In 2003, Jack Nicklaus and Gary Player, with the agreement of their players, declared a draw at the Presidents Cup when darkness set in on the last day and a winner could not be decided. It was the right thing to do. Golf is unique in that regard.

But with our game, we always wish we could do better. We are seldom completely content. And that wanting to do better, that desire, as the Buddha taught, leads to suffering or discontent. The Buddha advocated we stop desiring in order to end our suffering, but after many years of reflecting on this, I suggest that we do no such thing. I suggest that we continue to desire to do better, realizing that it not only can lead, yes, to suffering, but to joy and fun as well. If you squelch desire, you may also smother joy and fun. It's fine to moderate one's desires but not at the expense of joy and laughter or even at the expense of suffering, which can present tremendous life lessons leading to a deeper understanding of what it means to be a conscious human being. Overdoing desire, of course, can result in addiction, which is not a good thing. But overdoing the ending of desire can also lead to a kind of addiction: the conundrum of desiring not to desire, as Alan Watts once put it.

Golf is a great testing ground for this Western-style accommodation of an Eastern approach to life. The great Vietnamese Zen Master Thich Nhat Hanh advocates holding a half-smile at times, which could well apply to our capricious game. The other day, I watched Louis Oosthuizen, who often seems to have that equanimous half-smile on his face, hit a tee ball into the desert at the Match Play Championship in a game against Jason Day. He was dead in the water, er . . . sand and cactus, took a penalty drop from a poor lie, and struck his third shot on this par-5 first hole during his quarterfinals match. Day, I'm sure, figured he had the hole won, but Louis struck a 3-wood 270 yards to fifteen feet, holed the putt, thus making one of the most remarkable birdies I've ever seen. That half-smile never left his face as Jason missed his short putt to lose the hole. At no point did Louis say to himself, "I'm done. I'll never win this hole. I'm in too much trouble." He just took each shot as the mutually exclusive entity that it was, kept his mental attitude positive, and had fun with the game, staying present with the skills he knew he had, and let the chips fall where they may. That half-smile remained on his face even when he later lost the match (partly due to severe back pain), and shook Jason's hand.

So how do *you* approach a round of golf: with joy or with dread? If it's dread, you'll need to take a look at your relationship with the game. One great thing I've gleaned from the Buddhist approach to life is we are in close relationship with everything we encounter in life, especially that which we are passionate about. Whether it is your spouse, your work, your diet, your health, your children, or your play, what's important is whether it engenders joy or dread. What is the script you have in your head as you approach an encounter with any of those or a myriad of other aspects of life? This is why we have a certain mindset not only for entire golf courses, but for specific holes on that course. Again, dread or joy? We all have holes that fit our eye and holes that stick in our craw. We have holes we have scored well on, or have fond memories of; and we have holes we have yet to master, let alone score better than bogey or double on. We have these running stories going through our minds throughout life, and they greatly affect our approach to the trials and tribulations we encounter. We might feel a sense of dread when our boss approaches our cubicle. We might feel a sense of joy when our puppy greets us upon return from work in the evening. I dread the par-4 7th at Adobe Creek, where I often finish with a double. I love the par-3 5th where I had a one-in-one in 2013. But dread or joy, I keep coming back for another crack at it.

So how do you keep your attitude tractable and positive when confronted with these challenges that life presents? It is maintaining that half-smile in the face of inevitable change. And to sustain that smile, you'll need to concentrate on that which you have some control over; namely your swing, your course management, and your experience with each shot you encounter. Having fun with golf involves confidence and control. It involves an increasing sense of mastery, which you can attain over time with enough practice, patience, and proper instruction. When you're standing up to a daunting shot or hole, just be with your body, your stance, your breath, and your swing. That's the freedom you have, the potential joy you have, regardless of the troubling variables outside of you. While you're alive, the present moment is always there—this keystone of refuge, this bulwark of reality and relationship. Use it, and keep that half-smile intact, retaining your balance in the face of unwanted change. It's the secret to continuing to be at peace with golf, and life in general, no matter what the results.

Acknowledgments

NO WRITER IS an island, nor is any golfer. I'd like to thank those
who helped me write and promote this book via their inspiration, faith, and encouragement. First, my literary agent John Rudolph
who saw the potential and persevered until he found the right publisher. And that publisher is Skyhorse (love the name!), where executive editor Niels Aaboe ably guided this book's creation.

Favorite golfing companions, who keep the conversation on the
course energetic and edifying, include Rob Wallace, Steve Prebble,
David Tabb, Richard Schoellhorn, Patrick Tribble, Mike Beckett, and
Ed Biglin.

Thanks to the faithful readers of my *Mindful Golfer* blog who have
inspired and encouraged me since its inception.

Helpful golf instructors, coaches, and writers include PGA
Professional Jim Knego at Bennett Valley in Santa Rosa, Sonoma
County golf writer Bruce Meadows, my late coach Mike Marcase
at Overbrook High School in Philadelphia, my first teacher Oscar
Langman at a now-defunct driving range in Fairmount Park in
Philly, and my late coach Maury McMains at Drexel University in
Philadelphia.

Influential spiritual teachers in the Buddhist tradition include
108-year-old Zen Master Joshu Sasaki Roshi at Mt. Baldy, California,
Tan Ajahn Sumedho in Thailand, Joseph Goldstein at Insight

Meditation Society in Barre, Massachusetts, and the late Zen Master Seung Sahn in Providence, Rhode Island.

And special thanks to Michael Barkann for his support, my brother Hank in Philly, and, of course, my wife Ruth, who is always there with love, care, encouragement, and some great photo editing.